**Courtesy: Ohio Book Store, Cincinnati** *The Razor's Edge* W.

Somerset Maugham *Little Women* Louisa May Alcott *Light In August*

William Faulkner **Collection: Blue Hole, Cincinnati** *The Western*

*Lands* William S. Burroughs *Moby Dick* Herman Melville *Travels with*

*Charley* John Steinbeck *Brave New World* Aldous Huxley *Animal*

*Farm* George Orwell *The Cardinal's Mistress* Benito Mussolini *Don*

*Collected books for*
**The Figure as Fiction**

AF344274

*Quixote de la Mancha* Miguel de Cervantes *The Adventures of*

*Huckleberry Finn* Mark Twain *Vile Bodies* Evelyn Waugh *Robinson*

*Crusoe* Daniel Defoe *The Sun Also Rises* Ernest Hemingway *The*

*Mysterious Island* Jules Verne *Dr. Jeckyll and Mr. Hyde* Robert Louis

Stevenson *Resurrection* Leo Tolstoy **Collection: Joyce Howe** *The*

*Old Man and the Sea* Ernest Hemingway **Collection: Laurence G.**

**Stillpass** *Lily* Peter Feibleman *Whip Hand* Dick Francis

*Remembering Denny* Calvin Trillin **Collection: Christine Chronis**

*Possession* A.S. Byatt *The Volcano Lover* Susan Sontag **Collection:**

**Carolyn Krause** *Hotel New Hampshire* John Irving *Picturing Will*

Ann Beattie *Sherlock Holmes* Sir Arthur Conan Doyle *Saint Maybe*

Anne Tyler *Siddhartha* Herman Hesse *Neighbors* Thomas Berger

*Collected books for*
**The Figure as Fiction**

**Collection: Walter J. Sambi** *The Foundation Trilogy* Issac Asimov

*Imperial Earth* Arthur C. Clarke *2001: A Space Odyssey* Arthur C.

Clarke *The Hobbit* J.R.R. Tolkien *Lord of the Rings Trilogy* J.R.R.

Tolkien *Fahrenheit 451* Ray Bradbury **Collection: Elaine A. King**

**and R. Scott Farrow** *The Unbearable Lightness of Being* Milan

Kundera *Daniel Martin* John Fowles *Of Mice and Men* John Steinbeck

# The Figure as Fiction:

## *The Figure in Visual Art and Literature*

Presented with support from
Sirkin Pinales Mezibov & Schwartz
Attorneys at Law, Cincinnati

# The Figure as Fiction:

*The Figure in Visual Art and Literature*

Curated by Elaine A. King, Ph.D.

December 3, 1993 - January 23, 1994

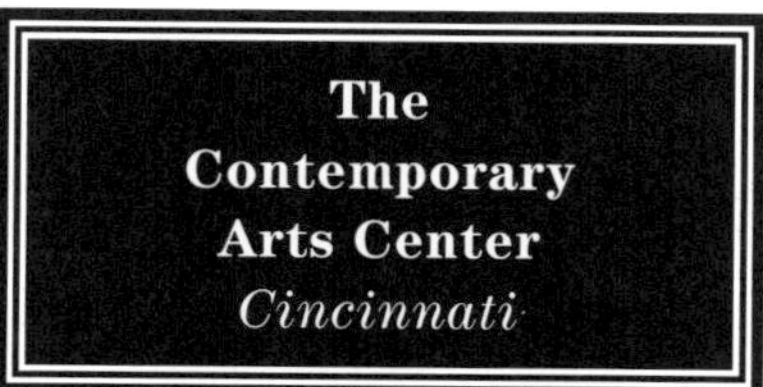

This catalogue was produced in
conjunction with the exhibition,
The Figure As Fiction: The Figure in
Visual Art and Literature,
presented at The Contemporary Arts
Center, Cincinnati
December 3, 1993 - January 23, 1994

© 1993 The Contemporary Arts Center
Cincinnati
First Edition
All rights reserved
ISBN: 0-917562-67-4

Designed by Steven McCarthy

Printed by Sidney Printing

*Photography Credits:* p.25: Photo by
Lawrence Beck, Courtesy Basilico Fine
Arts, New York, p.27: Photo by Jennifer
Kotter, Courtesy Ronald Feldman Fine
Arts, New York, p.29: Courtesy the artist,
p.31: Courtesy Sonnabend Gallery, New
York, p.33: Courtesy the artist, p.35:
Courtesy Betty Brothers, Covington,
Kentucky, p.37: Courtesy the artist, p.39:
Courtesy Curt Marcus Gallery, New York,
p.41: Courtesy Feature, New York, p.43:
Courtesy Postmasters Gallery, New York,
p.45: Courtesy Steinbaum Krauss Gallery,
New York, p.47: Courtesy Fawbush
Gallery, New York, p.49: Courtesy Jose
Freire Fine Art, New York, p.51: Photo by
Susan Einstein, Courtesy the artist and
Amy Lipton Gallery, p.53: Photo by Kim
Humphries, p.55: Courtesy Sperone
Westwater, New York, p.57: Photo by
Angela Cumberbirch, p. 59: Courtesy
Linda Cathcart Gallery, Santa Monica, CA,
p.61: Photo by Douglas M. Parker Studio,
Los Angeles, p.63: Courtesy Carl Solway
Gallery, Cincinnati, p.65: Courtesy Basilico
Fine Arts, New York, p.67: Courtesy the
artist and Michael Klein, New York, p.69:
Courtesy VAGA, New York via Leo Castelli
Gallery, p.71: Courtesy the artist, p.73:
Courtesy John Post Lee, Inc., New York, p.
75: Courtesy P.P.O.W., New York, p.77:
Photo by Peter Muscato, Courtesy
Feature, New York, p. 79: Courtesy the
artist, p.81: Courtesy the artist and
Elizabeth Koury Gallery, New York

# Contents

# Artists in the Exhibition

*Matthew Antezzo*

*Ida Applebroog*

*Martin Beck*

*Ashley Bickerton*

*Jay Bolotin*

*Darrell Brothers*

*Lesley Dill*

*Barbara Ess*

*Robert Flack*

*Sylvie Fleury*

*Rimma Gerlovina*
*and Valeriy Gerlovin*

*Elliot Green*

*Jane Hammond*

*Lauren Lesko*

*Paul McCarthy*

*Frank Moore*

*Daniel Oates*

*Tony Oursler*

*Ann Preston*

*Alan Rath*

*Michael Rees*

*Elaine Reichek*

*James Rosenquist*

*Amy Sillman*

*Megan Williams*

*David Wojnarowicz*

*Kevin Wolff*

*Pamela Wye*

*Lisa Yuskavage*

# Preface

I was honored that our new Executive Director, Dr. Elaine A. King, asked me to write this preface. A significant event in the life of The Contemporary Arts Center, *The Figure As Fiction: The Figure in Visual Art and Literature* is our initial intimation of King's vision of what is to be valued in contemporary art. The first indicator of her values is the title of the show itself. The art world has interested itself again in the figure as a focus for artistic expression. This certainly has not escaped King: with her many contacts in the art world throughout the United States and especially in New York, she has assembled a most impressive roster of artists and works for this show.

One point of interest is the manner in which the figurative image has returned to the fore after art's excursion into other realms. Another is the literary context, which provides material for comparison and contrast. Those conversant with the literature of magical realism as practiced by South American novelists and with the use of similar techniques in such films as *Like Water for Chocolate* and the very recent *The Piano* will not be surprised that mere representation is not the goal. Yet another notion is that the technological world in which we live affords many opportunities for experimentation in both medium and form.

For those who believe that art at its best crystallizes aspects of fully human experience, this show will provide ample material for enjoyment and reflection. Beyond the technological, *The Figure As Fiction* includes painting, sculpture, video, photography, and computer generated art. There should be something here for all of the broad-based, intellectually and artistically curious audience that comprises The Center membership.

We are grateful to the thirty artists represented in this exhibition for their participation, and for making our endeavors so rewarding. We thank Dr. King, who organized and spark plugged the exhibition, infusing it with her vision of what is best and most meaningful in contemporary art. The law firm of Sirkin Pinales Mezibov & Schwartz made a generous contribution towards the actualizing of Elaine's vision. The Center is extremely grateful for this firm's present and past support in a number of significant ways. We are extremely indebted to the collectors who agreed to part with their work for the period of this exhibition. We also are grateful for the assistance from the many galleries who represent the artists. These individuals responded generously to all inquiries and requests by Dr. King and her staff, and without their cooperation, the organization of this exhibition would not have been facilitated so smoothly.

While all members of The Center staff worked diligently, a few need to be mentioned individually. Karen A. Musgrove, Director of Development, worked hard to secure the funding for the show. Betsy Atzel, Registrar and Curatorial Assistant, displayed her characteristic attention to the many details involved in securing the loan of the works and in preparing for installing them. We continue to be impressed by the diligent work of Kim Humphries, our Preparator, and his technical crew, who did the unsung work of handling shipping and installation. Carolyn Krause, Director of Publications, performed the thankless task (for which we now thank her) of coordinating the essays, the design and the printing of this catalogue and patiently kept us all to deadlines. She was assisted by Lisa Schare. Steven McCarthy, catalogue designer, created the innovative concepts embodied in this publication.

As always, our thanks also extend to the entire staff of The Center. Moreover, my colleagues on the Board of Trustees have been doing yeoman service in caring for The Center and moving contemporary art in Cincinnati forward.

Anthony G. Covatta
Chairman of the Board of Trustees

# Prologue

*The student well advanced in Sherlockismus is aware, of course, that the earliest portrait of the detective now extant was not executed in oil, or crayon, or any of the other media artists use for pictorial representation, but was done in words, and by a word-painter of no mean talent. It is an arresting depiction, this sketch from life in black on white by the estimable John H. Watson, M.D., late of the Army Medical Department:*

*"His very person and appearance were such as to strike the attention of the most casual observer. In height he was rather over six feet, and so excessively lean that he seemed to be considerably taller. His eyes were sharp and piercing,...and his thin hawk-like nose gave his whole expression an air of alertness and decision. His chin, too, had the prominence and squareness which mark the man of decision."*

Walter Klinefelter
*Sherlock Holmes in Portrait and Profile*
Schocken Books

# *An Infinite Menu of Choice*
## *The Figure As Fiction*

We are living in a complex transitional time.  As a society we are bombarded by a morass of information, major technological advances, shifting international politics and economics, diminishing resources and life-threatening over-population.  In some ways, parallels can be drawn between our time  and the Industrial Revolution in the nineteenth century; both eras are marked by rapid, overwhelming technological and economic changes, with all phases of life being affected and altered.  In this Post-Industrial Age, the impact of the down-sizing of labor and the acceleration of the superhighway of information allow for myriad responses, both positive and negative, across global borders from Paris, New York, and Seoul, to Moscow, Madrid and Mexico City.

The Industrial Revolution brought human beings face to face with machines, a relationship that has accelerated and intensified throughout the twentieth century.  Today, technology permeates all areas of our environment. It no longer functions as a mere tool for advancement; it has become an integral part of every aspect of contemporary life.  Just as photography and film influenced all facets of the early Modernist movement at the onset of the twentieth century,  the computer, with its apparently unrestricted potential, is reshaping our lives and attitudes at the close of this Post-Modern era.[1]

The exhibition, *The Figure as Fiction* explores how artists at the end of this century are depicting the figure.  It presents a sampling of artworks in various media by a group of artists varying both in age and background. What they share is the necessity of coping with the flood of information that now overwhelms all of us.  How they integrate personal issues, observe reality and respond to external stimuli and cultural multiplicity is manifested in the art assembled here.  This work is clever and unconventional, and it requires careful reading.

Until the twentieth century, visual artists traditionally focused on the external, physical reality of the human figure, leaving it to literary artists to deal with the invisible aspects of human character and experience. The writers' words took their readers on voyages through emotional and geographical space, but it always remained for the readers to endow the fictional characters with a physical presence in their own mind's eye. In the visual arts, as in literature, there was always more than was immediately visible. For although one may think that one perceives visual works of art in an "all at once way," such works are often rich in symbolism, filled with implied messages and meanings that take time to decipher. Like literary works, such art releases its story over time.

The society created by the Industrial Revolution was one in which a growing middle class had both the means and the time to pursue leisure activities. Greater opportunities for education expanded the audience for literature and art. Books and prints became familiar items in many households throughout the United States and Europe. Reading novels became a popular form of entertainment and a status symbol. In both the visual arts and fiction, the figure was portrayed in a realistic manner through a formal, narrative structure. Since the close of the nineteenth century, however, and the rapid evolution of an avant-garde style of visual art embracing abstraction as its formal and dominant language, the figure in the visual arts has only recently returned to prominence. Just as James Joyce's *Ulyssess*, published in 1921, radically challenged the accepted order of fiction, so Marcel Duchamp ruptured aesthetic tradition by championing concept over retinal value. This master of the "Readymade" is credited with critically altering the direction of art in this century. In his work, the act of choice became imperative—objects unto themselves became useless outside the Idea. Like Duchamp, Joyce, too, can be viewed as a kindred-spirit to many contemporary artists who elect to mix metaphors and fragments, and act out of a posture of choice. As the book once entertained and influenced a society in the previous century, the depersonalized figure of the television and video screen has contributed to the comeback of the figure in art.

Although non-objective art tended to dominate mainstream discourse throughout this century until 1978, (when art such as that included in Marcia Tucker's *"Bad" Painting*[2] exhibition became known), figuration remained viable as a genre for both painters and sculptors, but in a less obvious and celebrated manner.  Appearing sporadically through the stylistic art movements of Surrealism, American Regionalism (Thomas Hart Benton-Brand and WPA) in the thirties, Pop, and Photo-Realism, in the sixties and seventies, it is only in the past decade that figurative art has once again gained a solid footing, divorced from a dependency on trendy styles or rigid theoretical validation.

Through the ideals of early Modernism, the avant-garde relieved artists of the traditional representational response to their world.  In each subsequent decade much art made during the past century was divested of extraneous subject matter through the process of subtraction.  Formal and material presentations were paramount—ethnic and cultural codes, as well as specific subject matter were progressively eliminated in the quest for a universal language.  After the devastation of World War II,  non-objective artists like Mark Rothko and Barnett Newman turned to reductivism in their pursuit of personal  spiritual paths.  In the sixties, the ultimate quest of Minimalist artists, such as Donald Judd and Robert Morris, to produce the perfect form and object led to an art that was cut off from the world and humanity.

Despite the explorations of Post-Minimalist and Conceptual artists, figurative art survived through the formal transformations of many late Modernists, including Robert Arneson, Chuck Close, Jim Dine, George Segal, and Robert Colescott.  With the rise of Neo-Expressionism and "Bad" Painting in the early 1980s, and with the work by a new generation of artists rallying around the work of Philip Guston, figurative art discovered a new vitality.  What separates this younger generation of figurative artists from those practicing prior to the eighties is their more conceptual and fragmented approach to the human form and its context, as opposed to earlier figurative representation which remained descriptively narrative and tied to the grid and art history. Although Pop Art and Super Realism rekindled an interest in subject matter throughout the sixties and seventies, it was the achievements of many—Jonathan Borofsky, Anselm Kiefer, Cindy Sherman, Leon Golub, Laurie Anderson, Nancy Spero, Ed Paschke, and Eric Fischl—who not only employed the human figure as a critical visual motif but also freely enlisted into their art a full range of human conditions, experiences, and knowledge.

In contrast, the figure in literature, theatre, film and contemporary culture has remained viably essential for decades. In the visual arts, figuration took a back-seat position as a significant motif. Now surprisingly, at the end of the twentieth century, the figure has returned to art almost one-hundred years after its slow demise, which began with the onset of avant-garde art under the banner of Modernism. During the past few years, academic and mediocre "politically correct" art have been crucial factors in restoring an interest in figurative art among both artists and audiences. Furthermore, the expansion of critical theory to subjects focusing on gender studies, multiculturalism, revisionist history, and ethnic identification has strengthened the relevance of the figure as subject. At the same time, the technological, imaginative world of *MTV* cannot be dismissed as insignificant; there is a strong, yet somewhat surprising media influence on the emerging artists of the "X" generation referred to as "Thirteeners."[3], a title assigned to the thirteenth generation of Americans born after the signing of the Constitution in 1776.

The term "figuration" is ambiguous. It refers not only to human or animal figures rendered in some recognizable degree, but also to the implication of figures in abstract works. Figuration manifested in American art since the eighties has taken on a new character. Instant communication and media access impact all aspects of daily life. An entire generation has grown up on television, computers and video. Today new technologies are as common-place as the telephone or electricity. For the first time in history, millions of people are able to see the same images and hear or read the same information almost simultaneously. An infinite menu of choice is now available to every-one—spectacle is commonplace and we seem to demand even more stimula-tion. Time becomes a critical factor on what is seen and how it affects the viewers and their ability to comprehend information.

A sense of fragmentation and transformation characterizes late Post-Modern figuration.  The figure in the nineties expresses the conditions of a fragmented social structure, conveying an air of suspicion, of fractured relationships and disfranchisement.  The portrayal of the figure has increasingly become divorced from representation.  Themes of denial, loss, cynicism, and identification have replaced the linear narratives of an earlier society that lived in a unified world of prescribed culture—gone is "The Age of Innocence."  The figure today no longer functions as a conveyor of factual essences,  but as a symbol or surrogate for other meanings.  An undefinable yet tragic tone prevails in much of contemporary art.  For some artists, figural references act merely as an extension of a performance, a mirror of culture, a window into another world, or as the proof for a critical theory.  However, the intention of the artist is no longer so obvious because the presented figure is often veiled and enigmatic,  and is no longer locked into a single category.

Because of the open-ended structure of this exhibition, a viewer may come away feeling frustrated.  This curator shares the expansive interpretations of the figure rendered by artists in all media.  *The Figure As Fiction* intentionally provides an assemblage—it gives no single definition of the figure.  The art presented in this exhibition neither constitutes a specific movement nor posits a particular ideological point of view.  If anything, this work shares a healthy diversity, from a quest for personal identity to a social critique of late Post-Modern society.  Today, the figure in visual art is more closely linked to the figure evoked in literature as a figment of our imagination. Because of society's exposure to multi-media, viewers today are capable of perceiving much information in a work of art without having traditional representation in front of them.  The visual artist, in a manner akin to the writer of fiction, now appears to produce the figure in an abstract way, more closely aligned to the way in which language builds a text.  However, unlike the writer who continues to be confined to the word in order to release concepts and narratives, contemporary artists now mix media and employ everything from painting and photography, to computer-generated art and video.  Many of the works included here are inter-disciplinary and cross-referential.

This exhibition is designed to allow each work to speak for itself. The idiosyncratic contents housed in the gallery could be equated with a library containing shelves of books spanning a gamut of genres—romance, horror, mystery, science fiction, westerns. In examining these works, viewers are asked to proceed with an open-mind and to allow the visual ideas to evoke narrative sensations prompted by their imagination. The artist does not intend to illustrate a single preconceived idea; but, instead, uses language to release an internal meaning rather than an external function or observation. An interesting  relationship can be discerned between contemporary art and nineteenth-century romantic and symbolist literature and painting. Through the use of symbol, metaphor and allegory, forms that represent one reality lend themselves to the expression of psychological, mythical and spiritual aspects of the human condition. As with fictional literature, a freedom for interpretation abounds. Just imagine two individuals sitting at a library table reading Flaubert's *Madame Bovary* or Sontag's *Volcano Lover*. Would the hero or heroine look the same in each  reader's mind? Would the same conclusion be derived about the author's intention or the hero or heroine's persona? It is doubtful! The same applies to the examination of Ashley Bickerton's recent totem self-portraits, which represent a composite of autobiographical symbols and elements.

Pop Art, and its "Five-Star General" Andy Warhol, burst the bubble on Modernist idealism. Since the early sixties, a marked shift can be observed in the sensibilities of Post-Modern art, which is marked by cynicism. Multiple readings and hidden agendas became common factors in this art, which deliberately set out to confuse and even irritate the viewer. Today, some artists attempt to skew dominant trends, and avoid making works based primarily on current mainstream theoretical discourse. As in the seventies, an atmosphere of pluralism pervades—artists have once again begun to engage in art-making in a declassified manner.

In examining this art, it is imperative to keep in mind that several generations of artists are represented. Many of the artists assert their artistic independence from the accepted culture but affirm a concern for ethical responsibility and shared values. James Rosenquist, whose career took flight in the sixties under the banner of Pop, explores powerful social issues in his recent paintings taken from photographs of mysterious, generic dolls. A strange sensation pervades these images that are at once ugly and beautiful, attractive and repulsive. Alan Rath is a young artist who uses his training as an engineer to construct sophisticated techno-sculptures in his investigation of the impact and implications of high technology on human life. Martin Beck's paintings, resembling pages from a story book, portray male rituals and bonding. But, what may seem ordinary or traditional, resonates as bizarre upon a closer look. Elliott Green is a member of the "Thirteeners,"[4] the generation of artists who grew up governed by media. His phantasmagorical compositions depict a curious blending of Disney cartoons with high art. This work demonstrates how values and attitudes invested in popular culture are vital subjects in contemporary art. Matthew Antezzo recycles photographic images used to illustrate critical reviews in New York art magazines from two decades prior—Barry Le Va appears to be engaged in the performance *Velocity*, 1970, "But what you see, is not what you think you see."[5] Applying a deconstruction approach to history, these conceptual paintings are not intended to read as simple records nor to celebrate Le Va—they are visual puzzles.

In the enigmatic images of Amy Sillman and Jane Hammond, nostalgia and memory come into play; the viewers are requested to examine the translucent layers containing collaged symbols and mythic characters. For them, visual clues function as a language in which visual signs may work to suggest nonvisual messages. Michael Rees reflects upon scientific advancements in the arena of genetics and human cloning. His bizarre sculptures of quasi-species, reveal his thoughts about test-tube creation and its potential consequences for future organic forms. Is this artist perhaps asking: "Has life become the latest artifact in global cultural advancement?" "Has the scientist become the great-sculptor-designer?"

The fictional drama in art by contemporary women often focuses on abuse, incest, and social scripting played out. Unlike feminists of the seventies, who sometimes blatantly asserted their disapproval of and anger toward male society through raw and sexual forms, some contemporary feminists opt instead to employ strategy, symbolism and critical theory in a more subtle manner. In the constructed paintings of Ida Applebroog, themes of isolation, violence and indifference are evident. Provocative theatricality emanates from her portrayal of human relationships and their fractured existence. Lauren Lesko's art is an exploration of female identity and a critique of the politics of sexual difference. Through her sleek conceptual approach, she emphasizes inherent aspects of female subjectivity. With a humorous bite, she addresses taboo zones in the life of a woman. Pamela Wye's computer-generated drawing/installation deconstructs the myth of Heidi and examines the expected female role of giver and nurturer. Her seemingly reader-friendly cartoon sketches pack a powerful punch!

A sense of hide-and-seek is evoked in the color saturated paintings by Lisa Yuskavage. An Edgar Allan Poe type of melodrama is conveyed by her images of solitary female figures; her women appear as mirages, standing seductively confident yet vulnerable. In the art of Megan Williams, old dictionaries are transformed into magical, three-dimensional, miniature landscapes through her careful carving. Williams uses the familiar book form as a point of departure in order to alter our notion of language and its hidden messages. Painting, photography and knitting—high art and craft—meet and meld in Elaine Reichek's explorations of gender and identity. In her *Tierra de Fuego* series, she demonstrates that the interpretation of a culture is dependent upon "who wrote it." A sense of heightened mystery characterizes the pin-hole camera imagery of Barbara Ess. With the absence of a depth-of-field, nothing separates shape and space; image and illusion are indivisible in her dark and haunting photographs.

Contemporary artists recognize that in the role of protagonist, they must address the concerns of the audience in an accessible vocabulary that relates their specific art to a viewer with shared experiences and cultures. In the highly formal collaborative works of Rimma Gerlovina and Valeriy Gerlovin, linguistics, mythology, painting, performance, sculpture and photography are explored in the pursuit of undermining traditional cultural values of words and objects. Visual and textual elements become interrelated but transformed in their paradoxical "photoglyphs." Daniel Oates accents the distinction between visual and conceptual through the use of familiar objects. His powerful employment of extreme scale holds one's attention: *Bella and Stella*, Hummel-like figurines, housed on a shelf, are contrasted with monumental, free-standing black work boots. Oates incorporates ordinary forms to construct assemblages that evoke a meaning not normally attributed to such banal subjects. Along the lines of the familiar, Tony Oursler's suited "wall man" endlessly chatters in a haunting tone; this simulated media character calls our attention to the way in which electronic machines are becoming surrogate human companions. The pervasive power of media and its ability to mold social thought and identity is called to mind in the exercise video installation by Sylvie Fleury. Humor, cynicism and fact come into play in this work that identifies the driving forces of fashion shaping contemporary culture and society's fantasy.

A renewed sense of social purpose and concern is evident in the works of Frank Moore and David Wojnarowicz. In his visionary but eccentrically realistic paintings, Moore subtly warns us about the AIDS crisis and the consequences of its many dangers through his use of careful symbolism. Although politically powerful, his work does not pontificate. The presented paradoxical visual elements are made seductively appealing by this artist's elegant use of glazes and sumptuous saturated colors. David Wojnarowicz's image/text poetic tableaux are visually and powerfully painful but spiritually rewarding. In his conceptual photographic poems, inner thoughts about life and eventual death are shared. The intertwining of text with images of decaying hands and skeletons embodies an authentic sense of self and of the power of the human spirit. The seriousness of the AIDS crisis looms large in Wojnarowicz's quiet but compelling works. Robert Flack is also a member the community devastated by AIDS and has suffered its damaging implications. At times, his art can be disorienting because of its subtle presentation of floating symbols in enigmatically lighted spaces. His work evokes a mystical and spiritual character that hints at an invisible world outside the realm of Western culture.  His visionary imagery celebrates the male body in an attempt to integrate the physical with the transformational tools of the mind.

The violence perpetrated within ordinary middle class families is the theme in the video performance by Paul McCarthy, who examines autocratic parents and child abuse through black-humor, hand-puppetry, and animation.

For each of these artists, the definition of art, the figure, the role of the artist, and even the meaning of the viewer's gaze, varies greatly.  This dynamic combination of artworks by established and emerging artists was chosen deliberately in order to cast a wide net.  In some instances, the artist intends the figure to represent an aesthetic end in itself.  In other examples, the figure might function as metaphor, intended to convey complex psychological, emotional, and critical investigations, either about the artist personally or about the larger society in which he/she lives and works.  We hope that the viewer will see not only wherein the "figure is fiction" but also where it is fact. Novels were not written in a vacuum...have we not all encountered a Scarlett, even though the "Old South," and Tara are long gone?

Elaine A. King, Ph.D.
Executive Director  and Chief Curator

*End Notes*

1.  The author of this essay has for several years been exploring the effects of advanced technology and its impact on human life.  This exhibition is a continuation of that investigation.  The exhibition, *Art in the Age of Information*, exhibited from February through March 1993, at the Wood Street Galleries of the Pittsburgh Cultural Trust, was the first visual manifestation of this theme.  The forthcoming exhibition, INTERFORMATION, planning to open sometime in 1995, will further analyze this subject.  Artists, through their work,  provide a valuable visual barometer about humanity.

2.  *"Bad" Painting*, curated by Marcia Tucker, was exhibited at the New Museum, New York, January 14 - February 28, 1978.

3.  Neil Howe and William Strauss, "The New Generation Gap," *The Atlantic Monthly*, vol. 270, no. 6, December 1992, p. 68.

4.  Ibid.

5.  This reference is parody  inspired by  a quote from Frank Stella, who, when asked about his art replied, "What you see, is what you see."

# Works in the Exhibition

# Matthew Antezzo

***Arts, Sept. 1971, p. 40, 1993***

*oil on canvas*

64 x 46

Courtesy:  Basilico Fine Arts, New York

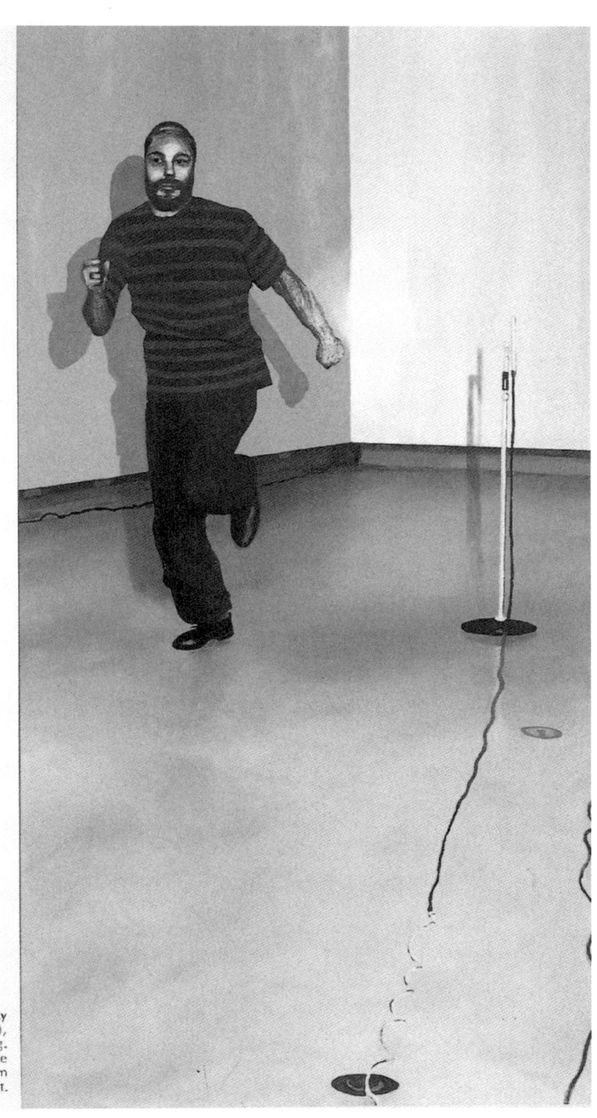

Barry LeVa, Velocity Piece #2 (1970), artist running. Courtesy of the La Jolla Museum of Art.

# Ida Applebroog

*orgiastic/romantic plastic, 1990*

*oil on canvas*

90 x 128

Courtesy:  Ronald Feldman Fine Arts,

New York

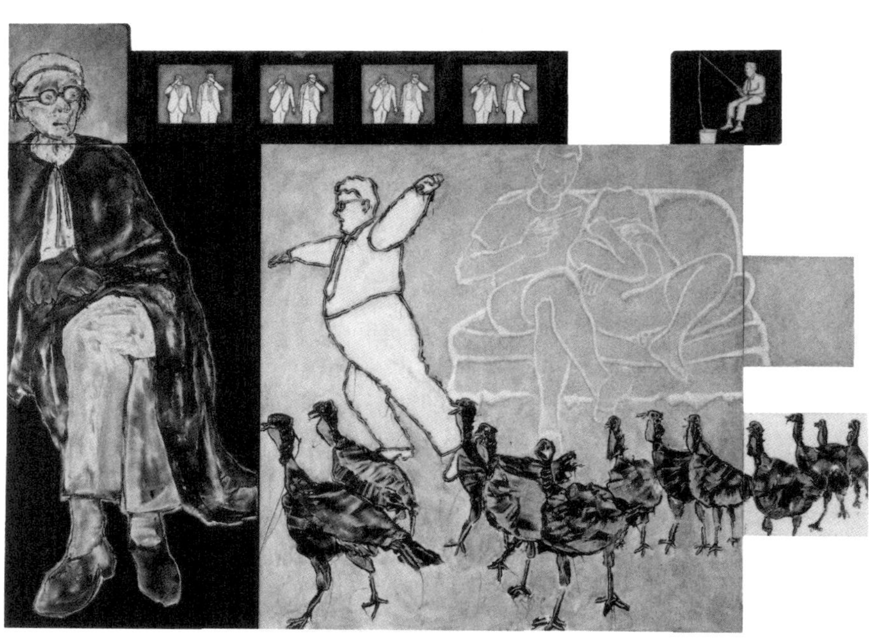

# Martin Beck

*Orchestration, 1993*

*oil on canvas*

59 x 49

Courtesy:  Artist,

Jersey City, New Jersey

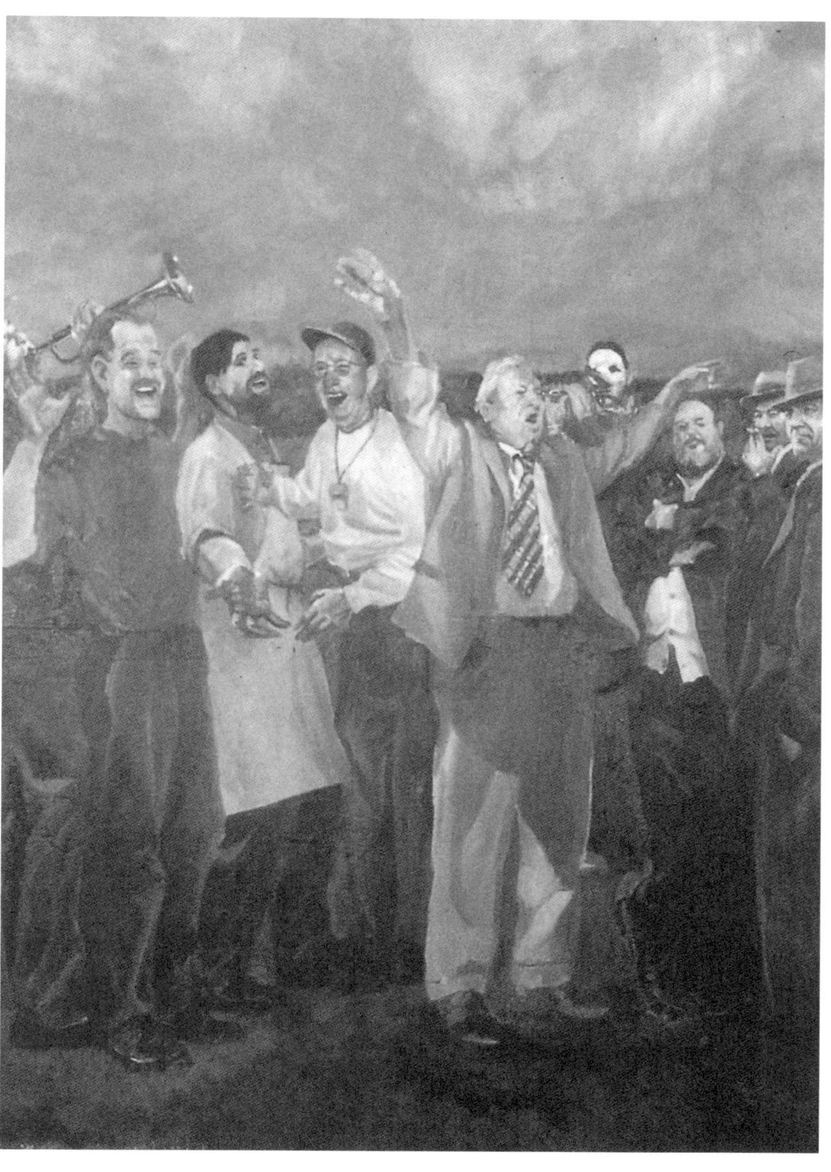

# Ashley Bickerton

***Self Portrait:***

***Desert Island Head, 1993***

*translucent turquoise rubber head,*

*dyed human hair, steel, coconuts,*

*river rocks*

85 1/2 x 14 x 9 1/2

Courtesy: Sonnabend Gallery,

New York

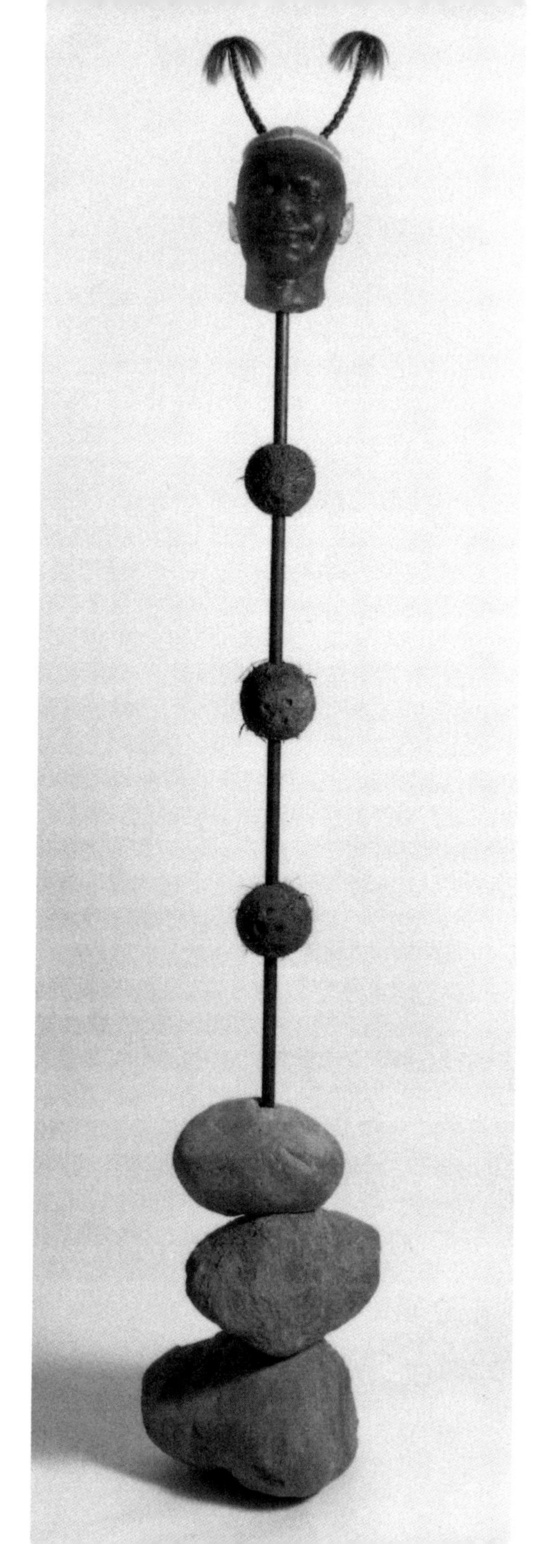

**Jay Bolotin**

***The Drummer, 1993***

*oil on wood panel*

41 1/2 x 36 x 2

Courtesy:  Artist, Cincinnati

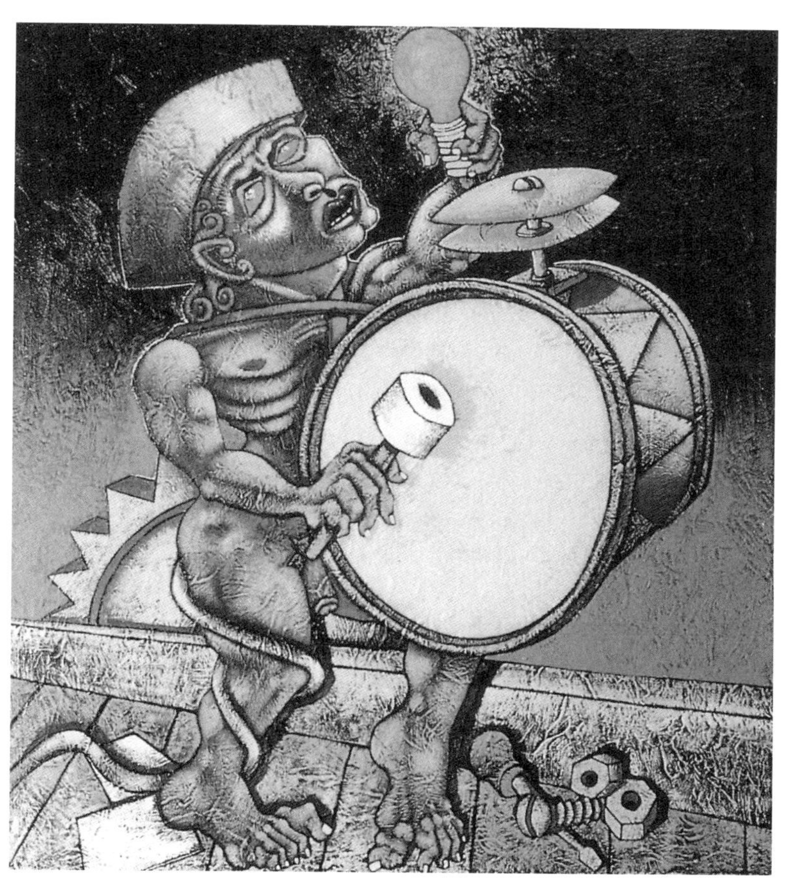

# Darrell Brothers

**#3, 1981**

*liquatex on canvas*

86 x 66

Collection:  Betty Brothers,

Covington, Kentucky

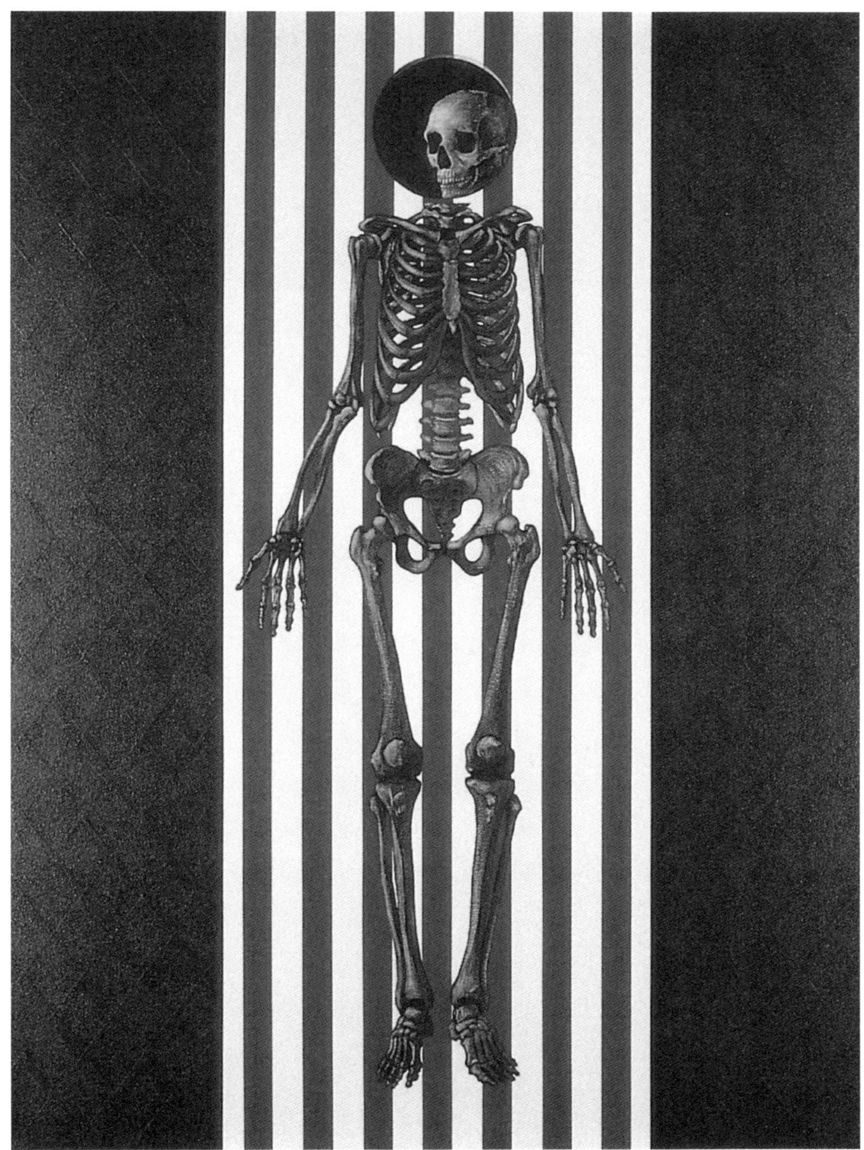

***White Hinged Poem Dress #2, 1993***

*mixed media, wire armature*

34 3/4 x 21 x 14

Courtesy:  Patricia Shea Gallery,

Santa Monica

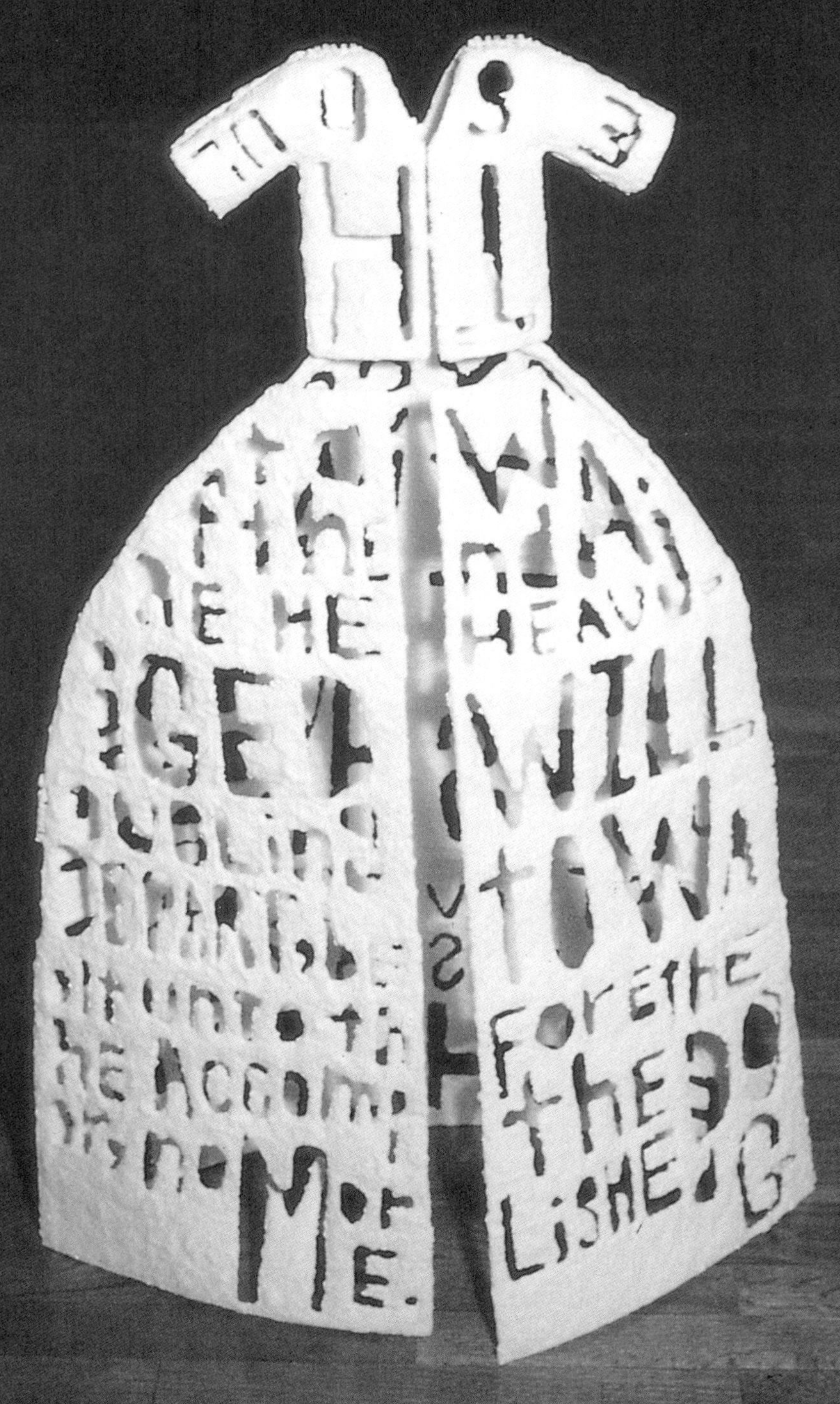

# Barbara Ess

***Untitled (Barbie Doll, BE 2201), 1991***

*color photograph*

50 x 69

Courtesy:  Curt Marcus Gallery, New York

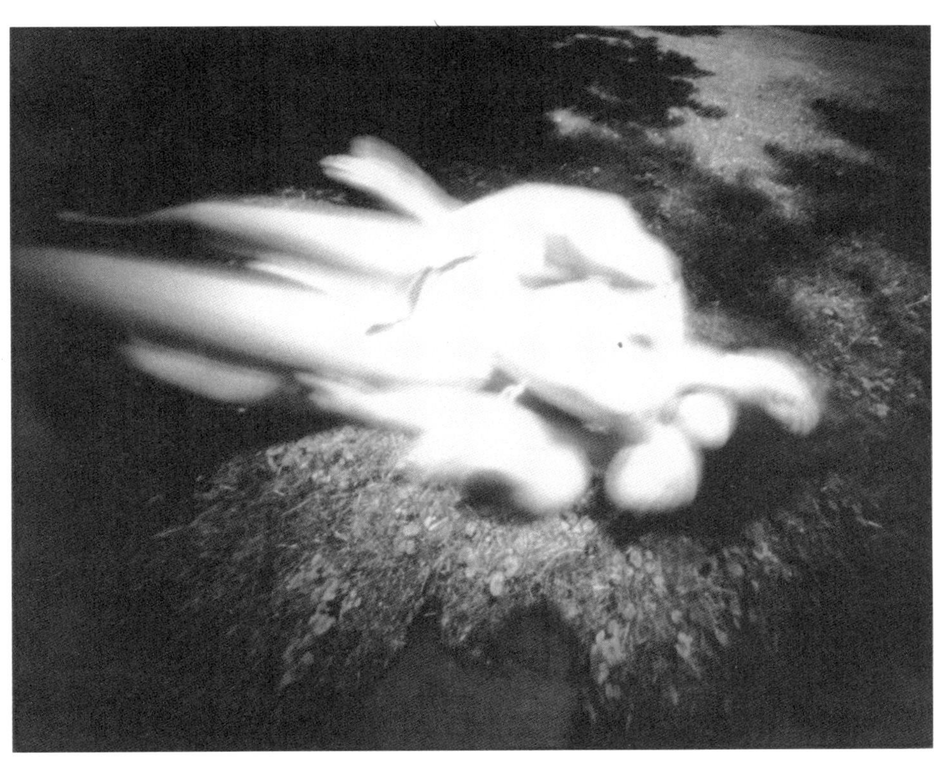

# Robert Flack

***Portal, 1990***

*c-print*

40 x 30

Estate of Robert Flack

Courtesy:  Feature, New York

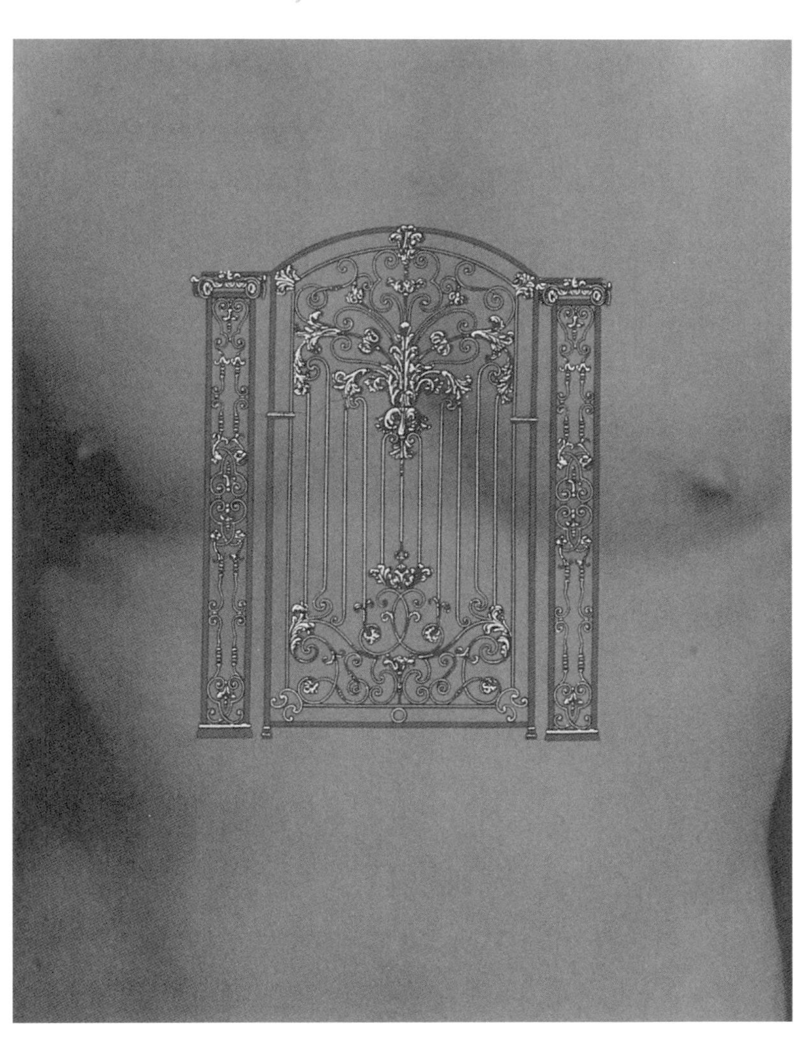

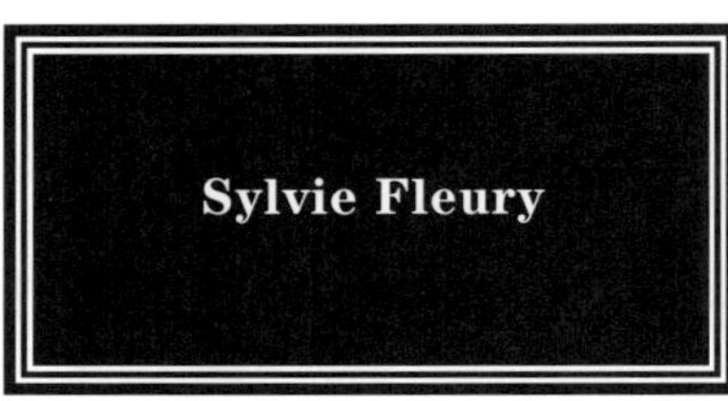


***Journey to Fitness or How to Lose 10 Pounds in 3 Weeks, 1993***

*seven video tapes, VCR, television monitors*

42 x 80 x 60

Collection:  Robert J. Shiffler,

Greenville, Ohio

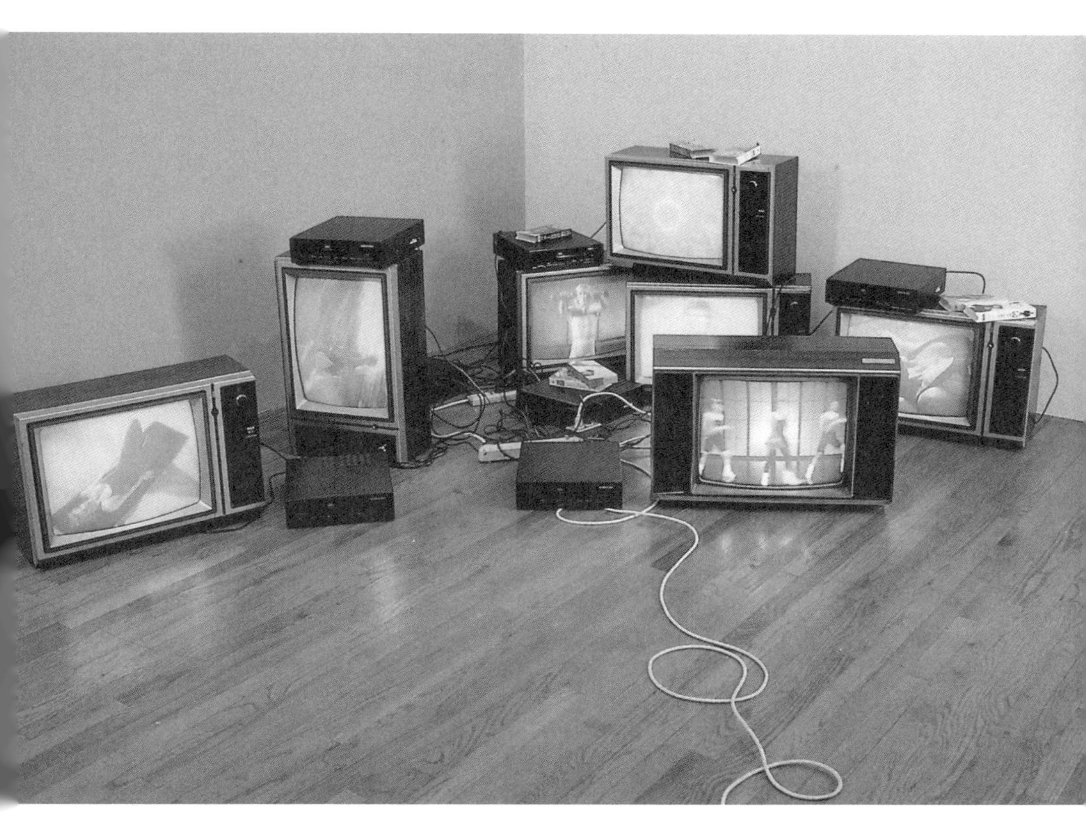

*To Be, 1989*

*ektacolor print*

48 x 48

Courtesy:  Steinbaum Krauss Gallery,

New York

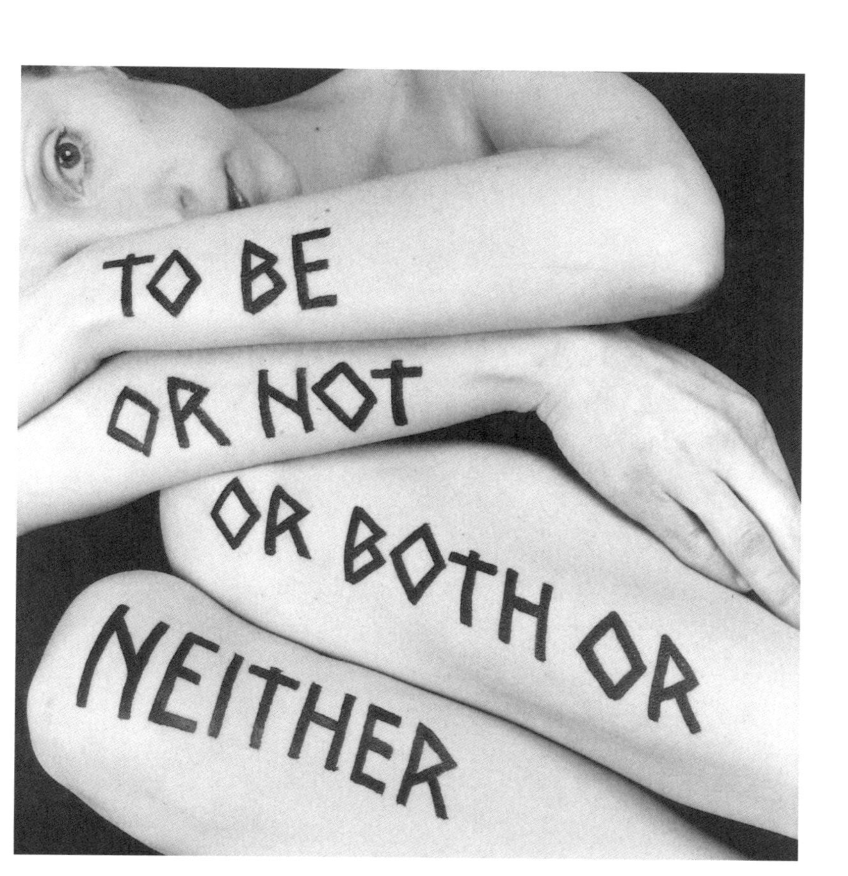
TO BE
OR NOT
OR BOTH OR
NEITHER

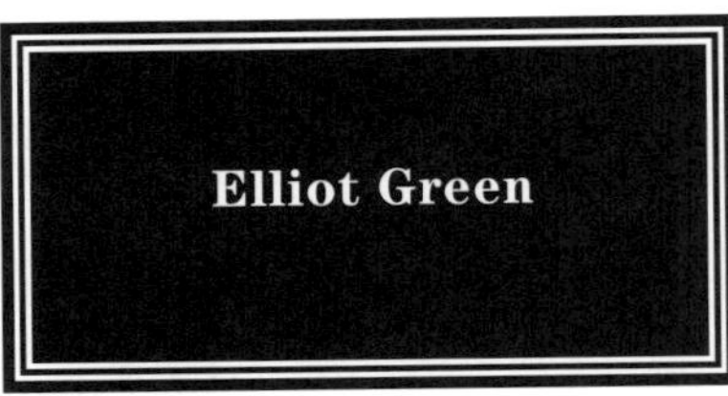


**Emergence #49, 1993**

*oil on canvas*

24 x 36

Courtesy:  Fawbush Gallery, New York

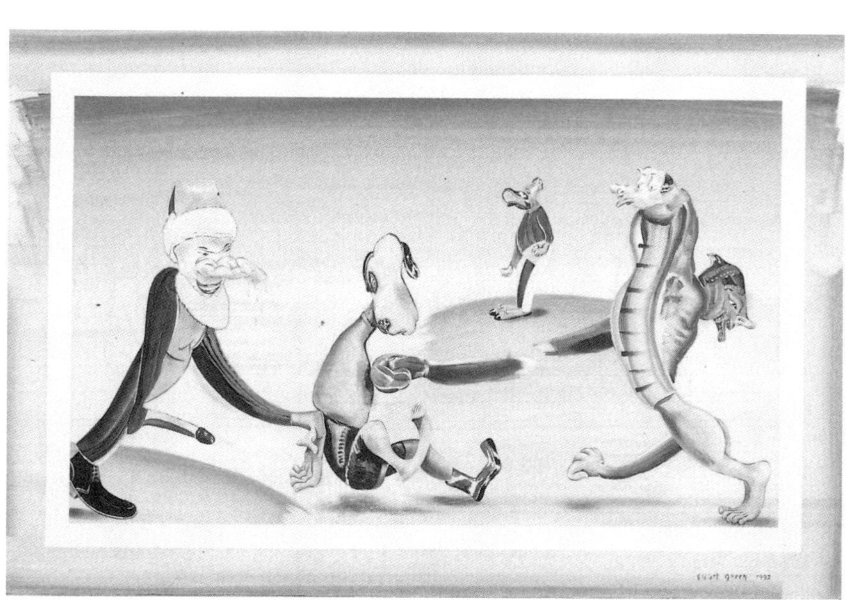

**Jane Hammond**

***Science and Sound, 1993***

*graphite, crayon, colored pencil,*

*color xerox transfers, linoleum block,*

*gouache and acrylic on rice paper*

35 1/2 x 32 1/2

Private Collection:  Orlando, Florida

Courtesy:  Jose Freire Fine Art Inc.,

New York

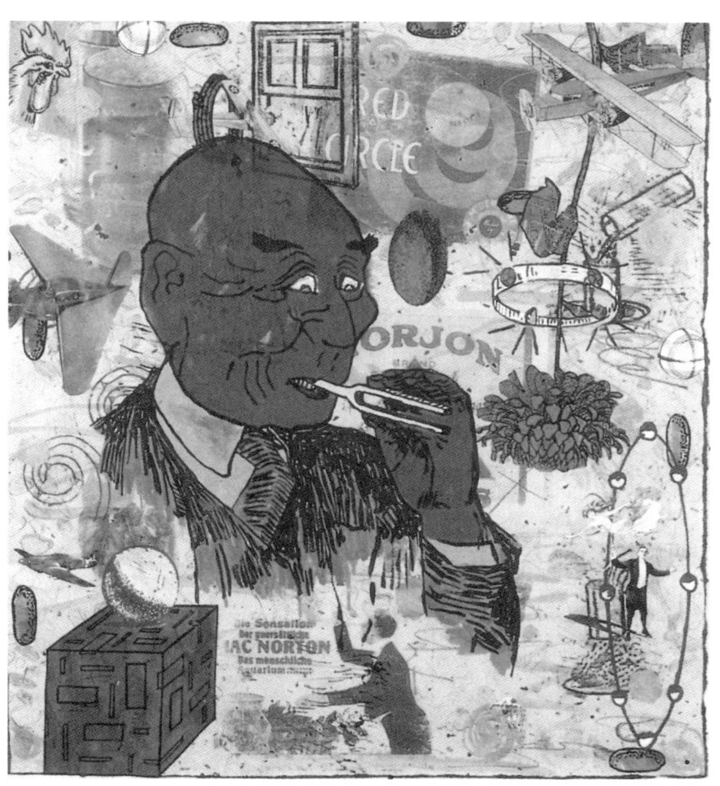
RED
CIRCLE
NORJON
BRAND
Die Sensation
der vorstehende
MAC NORTON
Das menschliche
Aquarium heißt

*Orifice (1 of 9), 1991*

*leather and embroidered text*

8 x 8 x 4

Courtesy:  Artist, Los Angeles and

The Lipton Owens Company, New York

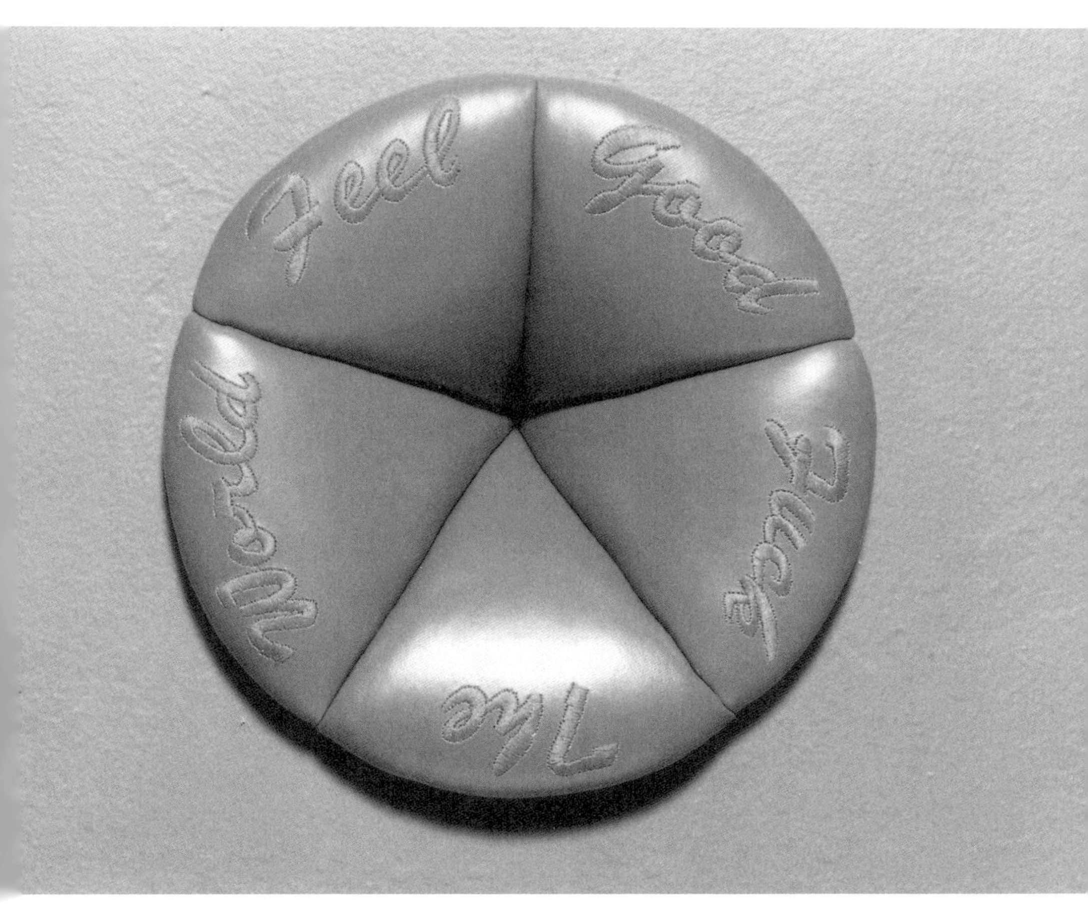

Feel
Good
Keep
The
World

**Paul McCarthy**

***Cultural Soup, 1987***

*still from video installation*

25 minutes

Courtesy:  Artist, New York and

Rosamund Felsen Gallery, Los Angeles

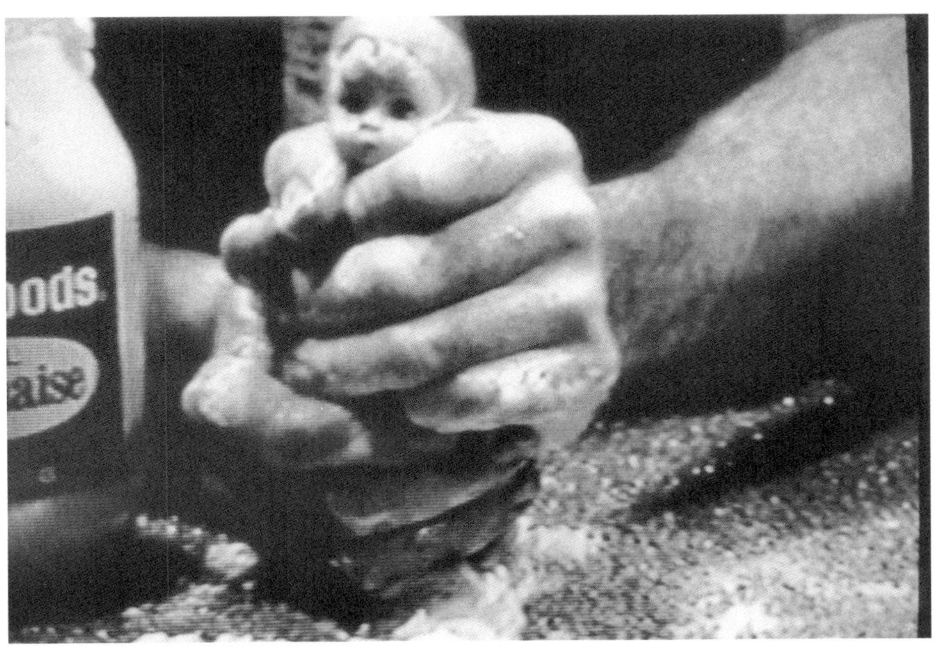
ods.
aise

# Frank Moore

***Country Club, 1992***

*oil on canvas with attachments*

34 x 28

Collection:  Gian Enzo Sperone,

New York

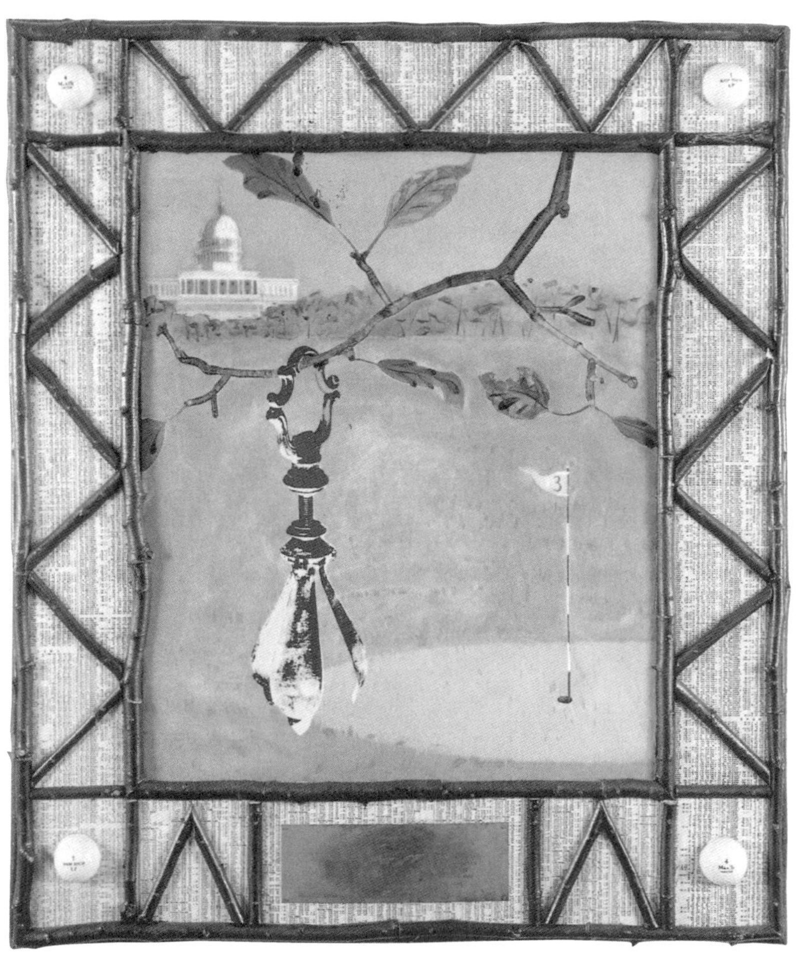

# Daniel Oates

***Happy Workers (Bella and Stella),***

***1992***

*rigid urethane and acrylic paint*

5 x 8 5/8 x 5

Collection:  Arthur G. Rosen,

Wayne, New Jersey

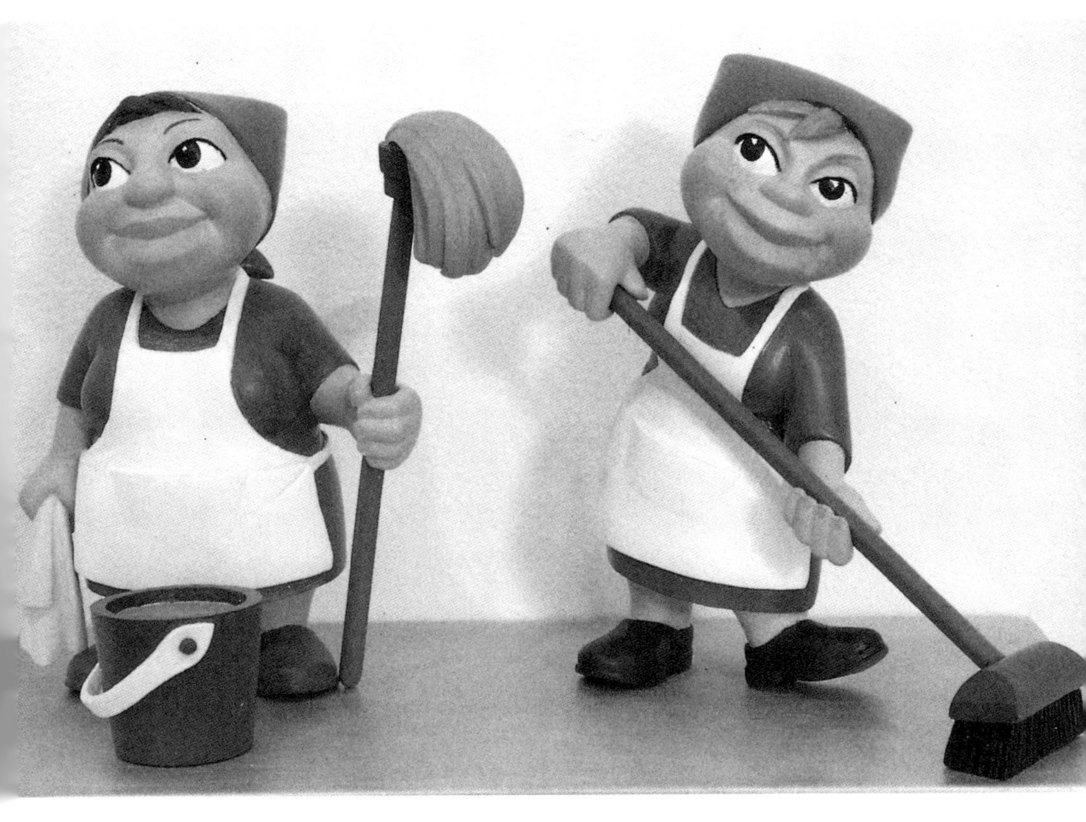

# Tony Oursler

**Road Movie II, 1993**

*mixed media*

dimensions variable

Courtesy:  Linda Cathcart Gallery,

Santa Monica

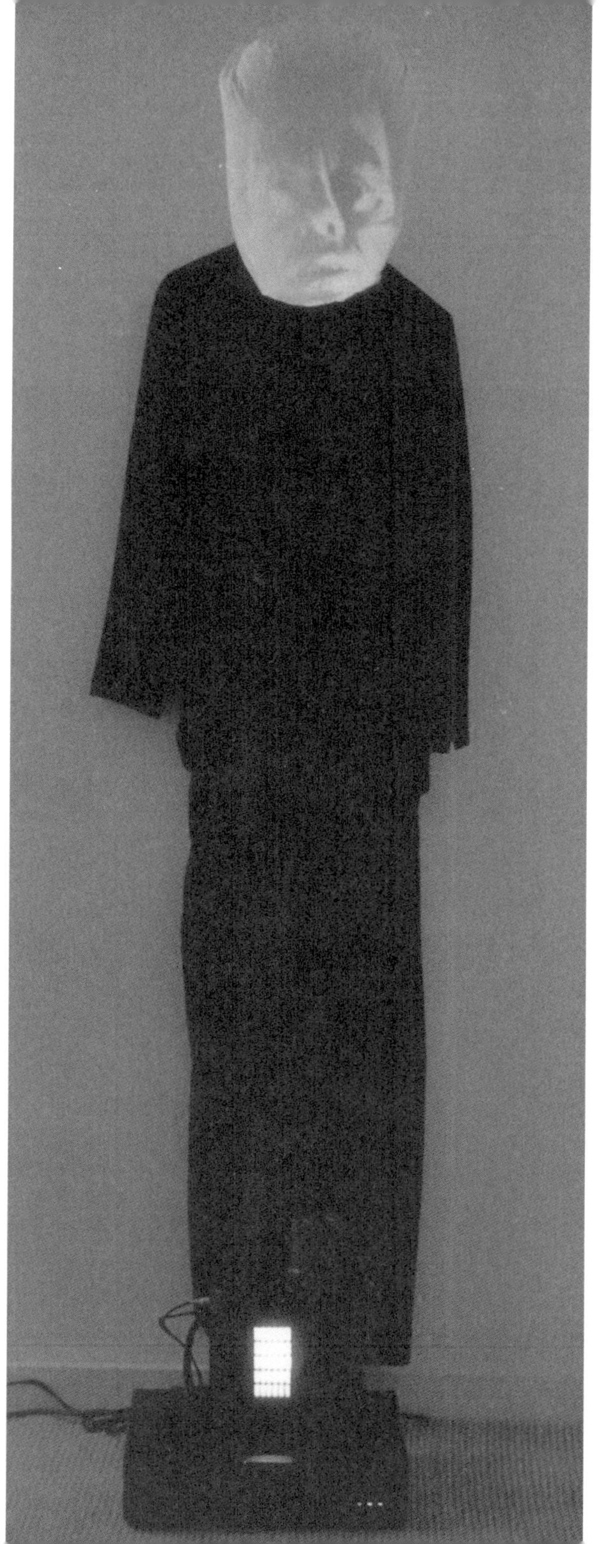

# Ann Preston

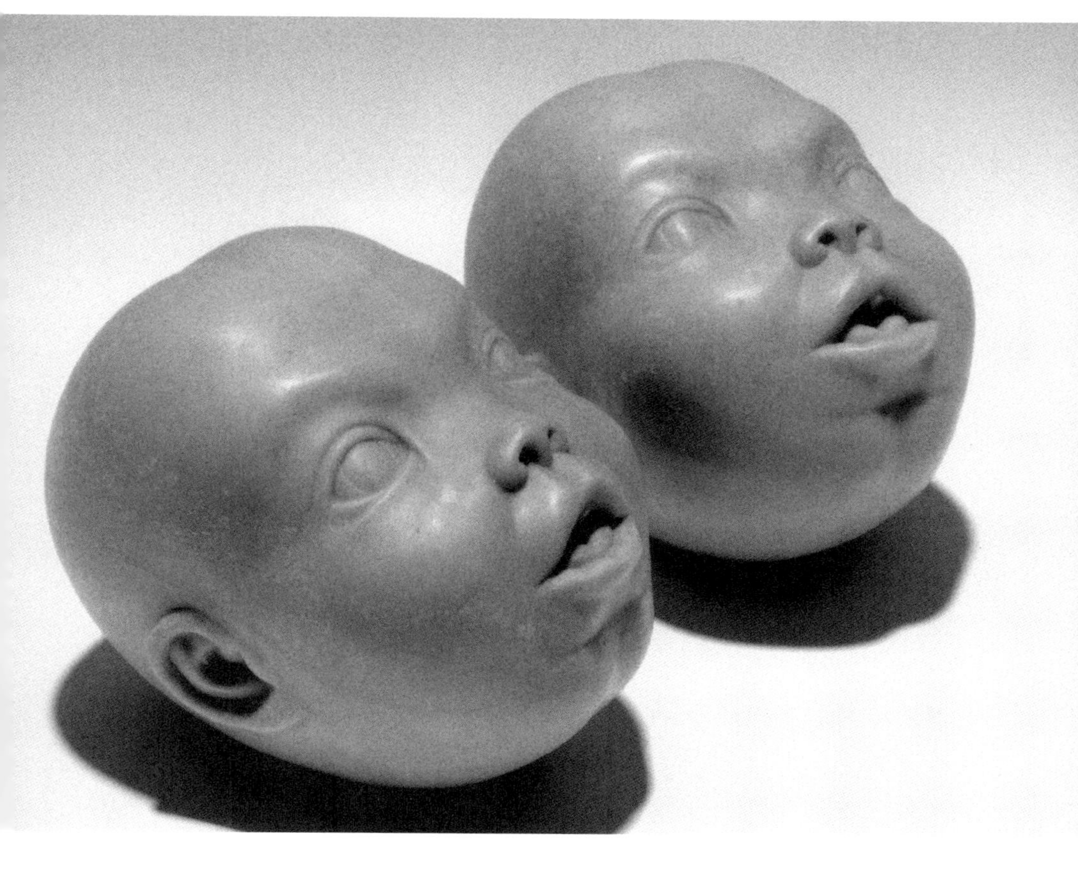

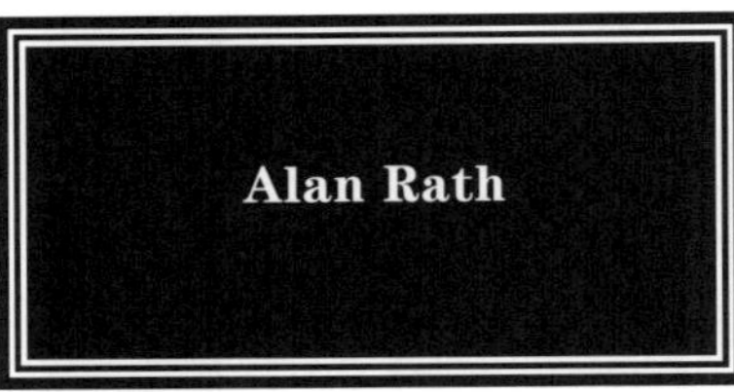



***Maya's Mikoshi, 1992***

*electronics, aluminum, 5 cathode ray tubes*

96 x 56 x 29

Collection:  Robert J. Shiffler,

Greenville, Ohio

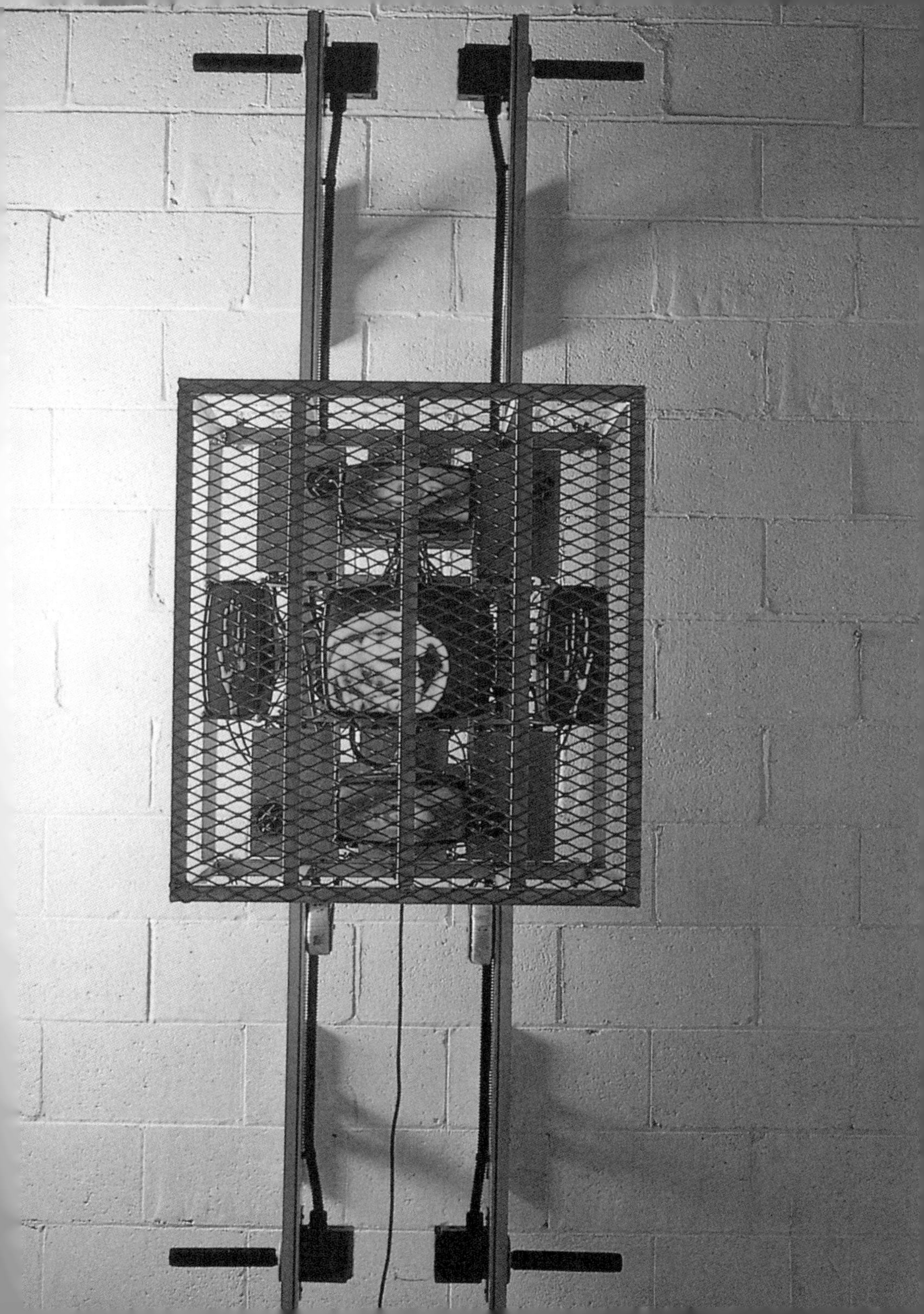

## Michael Rees

***Untitled, 1992***

*concrete and plastic composites*

12 x 12 1/2 x 19

Private Collection:  Cincinnati

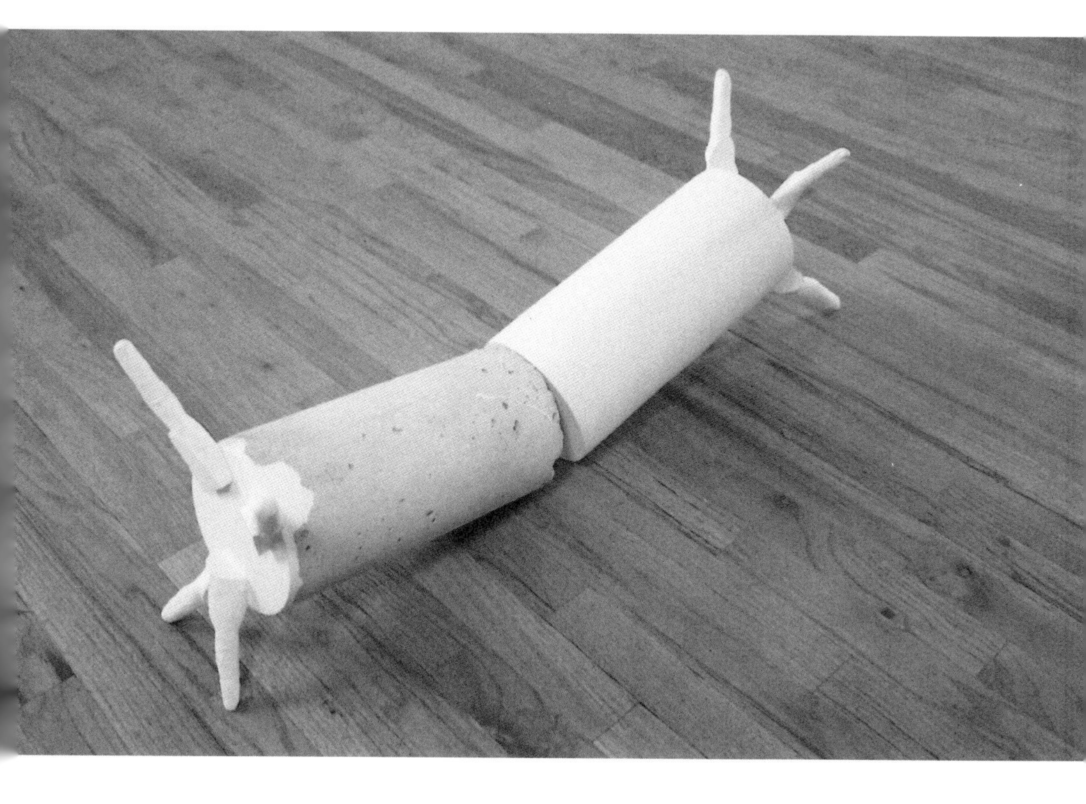

# Elaine Reichek

***Blue Men, 1986***

*photograph, wool*

63 x 96

Courtesy:  Artist and Michael Klein Inc.,

New York

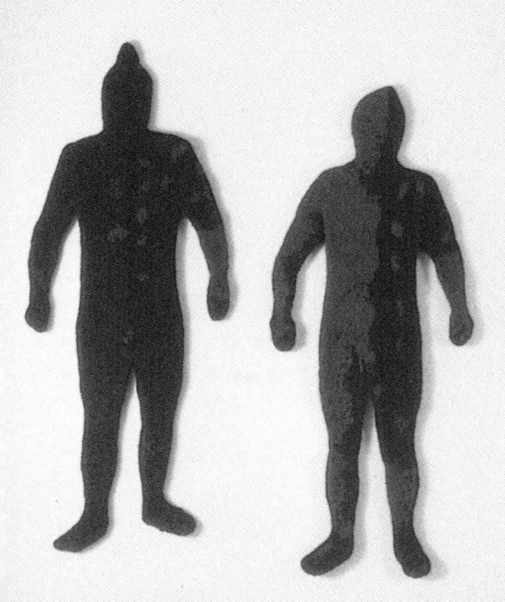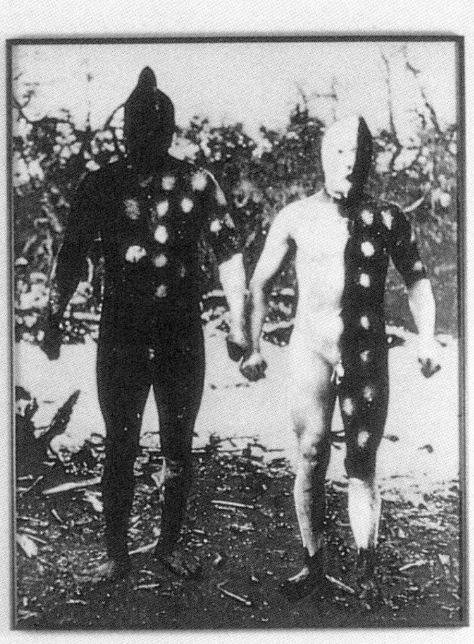

**James Rosenquist**

***Gift Wrapped Doll #4 (307), 1992***

*oil on canvas*

60 x 60

Courtesy:  Leo Castelli Gallery, New York

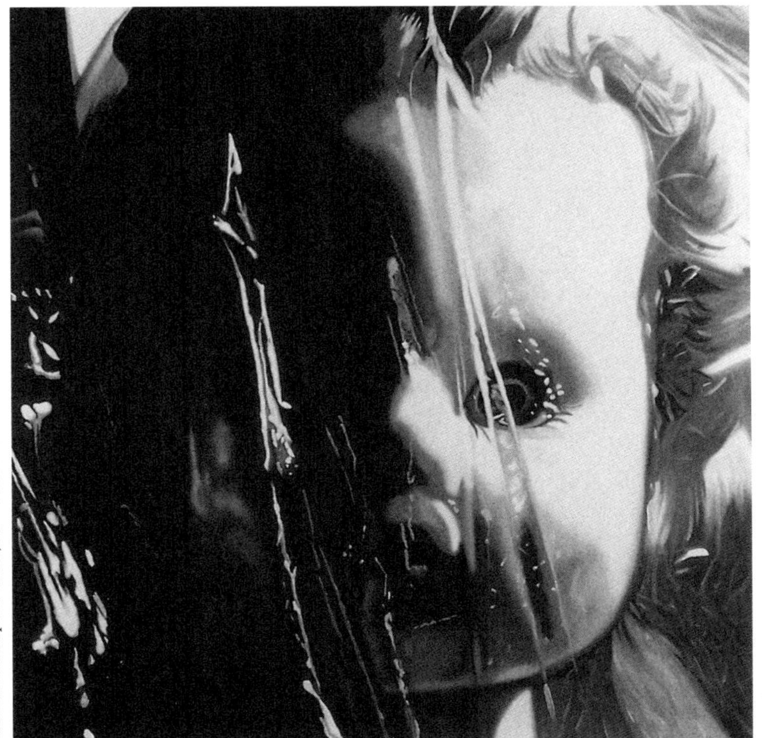

**Amy Sillman**

**Bad Dog, 1993**

*oil, ink, gouache on wood*

48 x 48

Courtesy:  Salvatore Ala Gallery,

New York

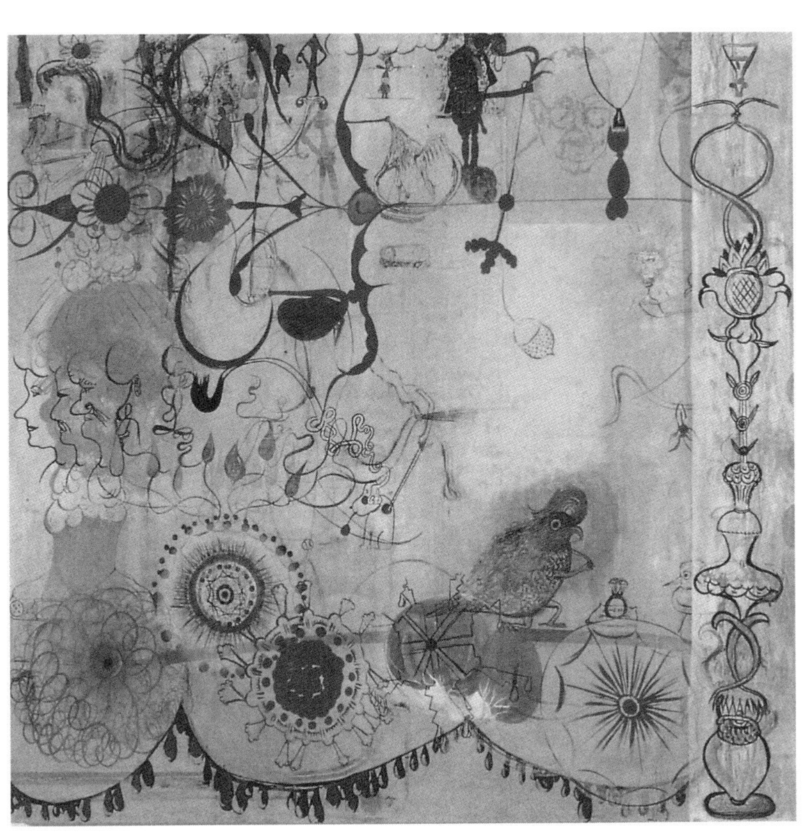

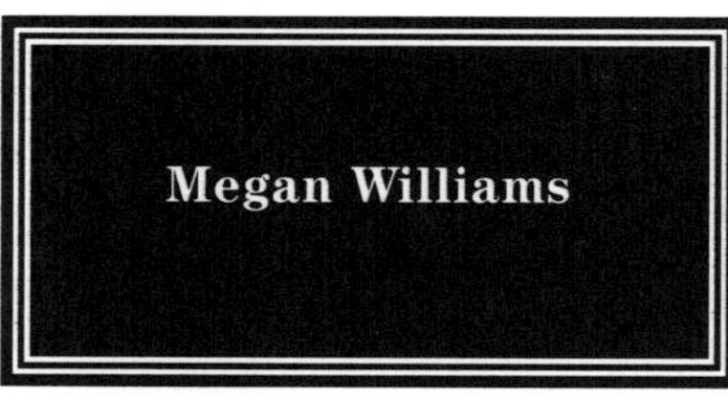



**Untitled (Large Blue Dictionary), 1992**

*altered book on pedestal*

4 x 8 1/2 x 11

Courtesy:  John Post Lee Gallery, New York

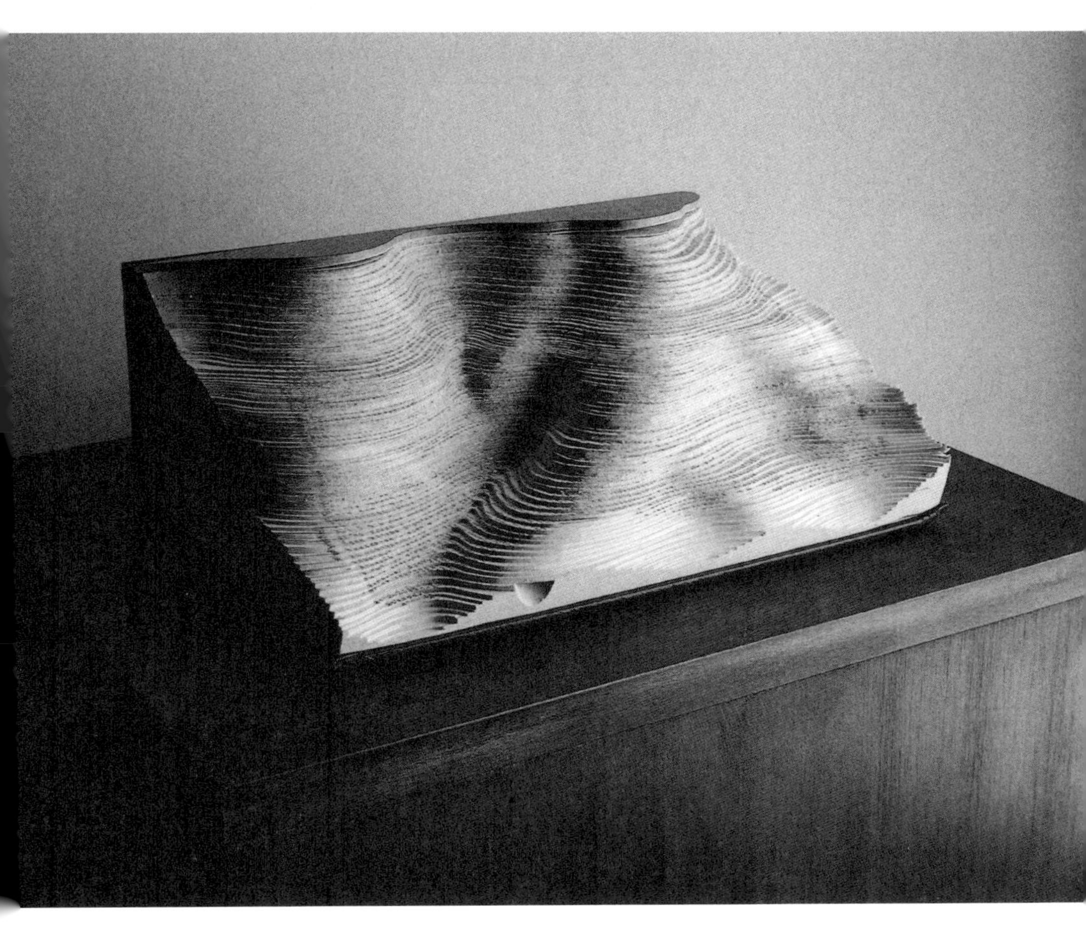

*"When I Put My Hands on Your Body...",*

*1990*

*silkscreen on photograph*

26 x 38

Courtesy:  P.P.O.W., New York

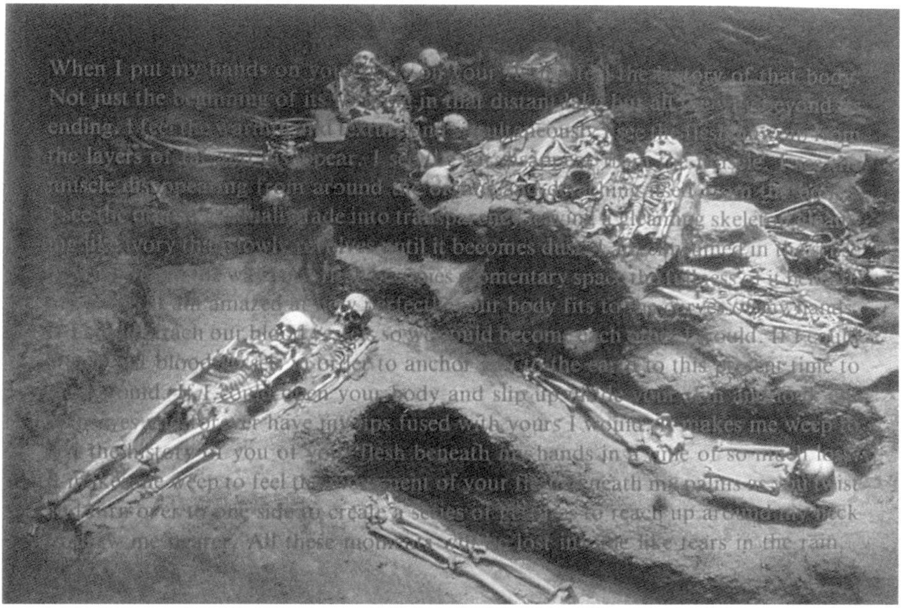

When I put my hands on your body on your flesh I feel the history of that body. Not just the beginning of its forming in that distant lake but all the way beyond its ending. I feel the warmth and texture and simultaneously I see the flesh unwrap from the layers of fat and disappear. I see the fat disappear from the muscle. I see the muscle disappearing from around the organs and detaching itself from the bones. I see the organs gradually fade into transparency leaving a gleaming skeleton gleaming like ivory that slowly turns dust until it becomes dust and then floating in open space. I see the shape of your body fades and creates momentary space that the wind passes through. I am amazed at how perfectly your body fits to the curves of my hands. If I could attach our blood vessels so we could become each other I would. If I could attach our blood vessels in order to anchor you to the earth to this present time to keep you from this slow death I would. If I could open up your body and slip up inside your skin and look out your eyes and forever have my lips fused with yours I would. It makes me weep to feel the history of you of your flesh beneath my hands in a time of so much loss. It makes me weep to feel the movement of your flesh beneath my palms as you twist and turn over to one side to create a series of gestures to reach up around my neck to draw me nearer. All these moments will be lost in time like tears in the rain.

**Kevin Wolff**

***Arm with Hole, 1991***

*acrylic on canvas*

42 x 80

Collection:  Neuberger and Berman,

New York

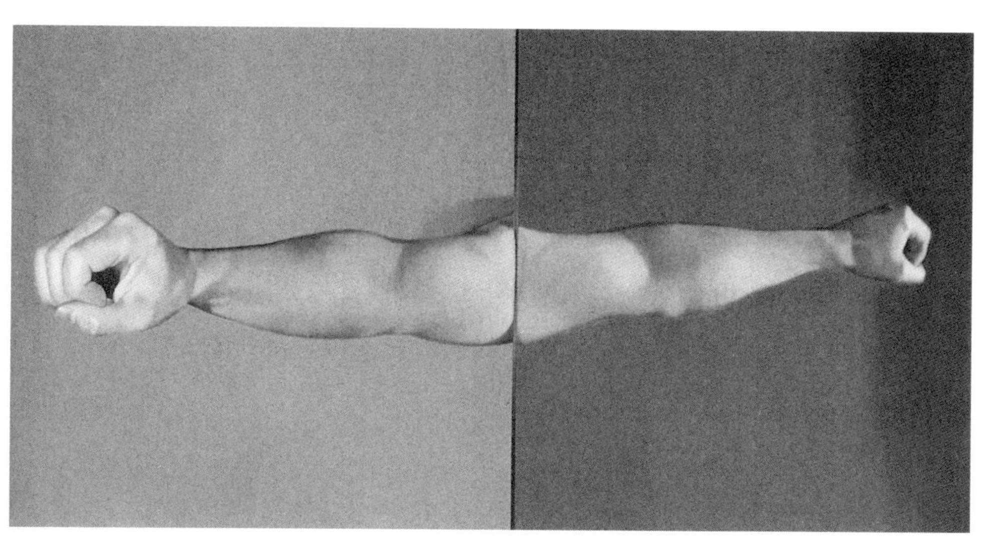

**Pamela Wye**

***Heidiology, (detail) 1993***

*57 @ 8 1/2 x 11" computer images on paper*

96 x 72

Courtesy:  Artist, New York

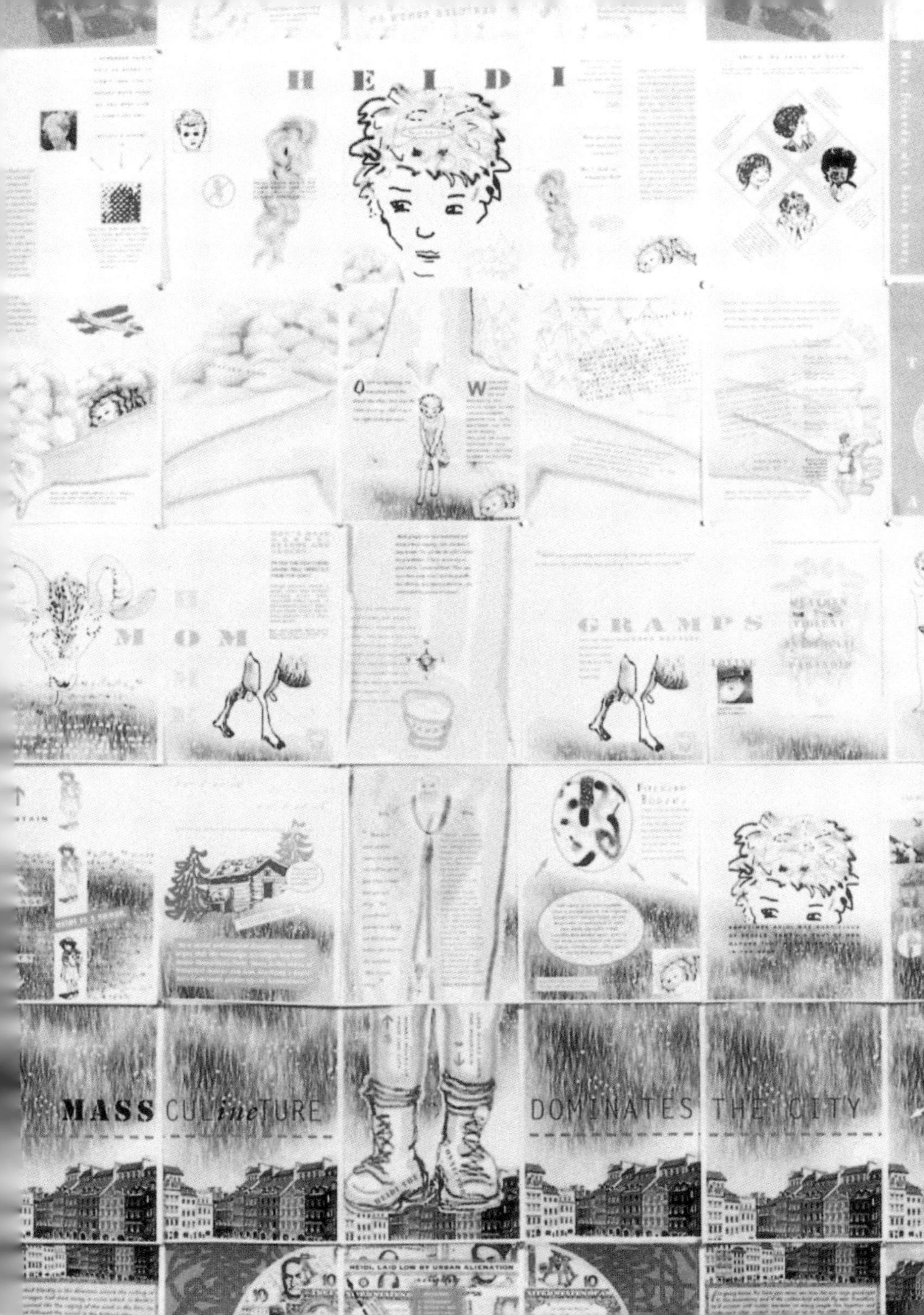
HEIDI
MOM
GRAMPS
MASS CULineTURE DOMINATES THE CITY
HEIDI, LAID LOW BY URBAN ALIENATION

# Lisa Yuskavage

*Big Marie, 1993*

*oil on linen*

64 x 50 x 2

Courtesy:  Artist and

Elizabeth Koury Gallery, New York

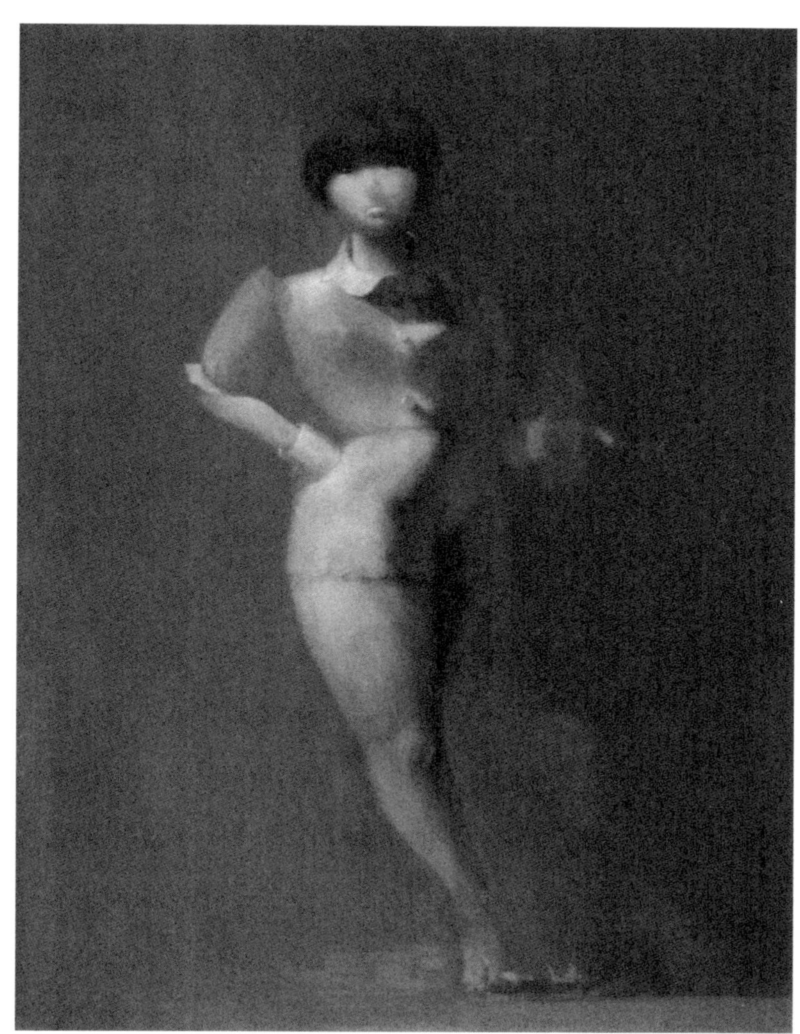

# Checklist of the Exhibition

*Dimensions are in inches. Height precedes width precedes depth.*

## Matthew Antezzo

***Artforum, Feb. 1973, p. 45, 1993***
*oil on canvas*
65 x 50
Collection: Jederman, N.A.
Courtesy: Basilico Fine Arts, New York

***Arts, Sept. 1971, p. 40, 1993***
*oil on canvas*
64 x 46
Courtesy: Basilico Fine Arts, New York

## Ida Applebroog

***orgiastic/romantic plastic, 1990***
*oil on canvas*
90 x 128
Courtesy: Ronald Feldman Fine Arts, New York

## Martin Beck

***Orchestration, 1993***
*oil on canvas*
59 x 49
Courtesy: Artist, Jersey City, New Jersey

## Ashley Bickerton

***Self Portrait: Desert Island Head, 1993***
*translucent turquoise rubber head, dyed human hair, steel, coconuts, river rocks*
85 1/2 x 14 x 9 1/2
Courtesy: Sonnabend Gallery, New York

***Self Portrait: Kelapa-Kepala, 1993***
*translucent turquoise rubber head, dyed human hair, steel, plaster, enamel*
88 1/2 x 12 x 11
Courtesy: Sonnabend Gallery, New York

## Jay Bolotin

***Working Libretto for Limbus Fatuo Rum, 1993***
*ink over words of Lewis Carroll's Alice in Wonderland*
11 x 8 x 1
Collection: Artist, Cincinnati

***The Drummer, 1993***
*oil on wood panel*
41 1/2 x 36 x 2
Courtesy: Artist, Cincinnati

***Secunda, Lucy, and the Baby Brother, 1993***
*oil on wood panel*
41 1/2 x 36 x 2
Courtesy: Artist, Cincinnati

## Darrell Brothers

*#3, 1981*
*liquatex on canvas*
86 x 66
Collection: Betty Brothers, Covington,
Kentucky

## Lesley Dill

*White Hinged Poem Dress #2, 1993*
*mixed media, wire armature*
34 3/4 x 21 x 14
Courtesy: Patricia Shea Gallery,
Santa Monica

## Barbara Ess

*Untitled (Barbie Doll, BE 2201),
1991*
color photograph
50 x 69
Courtesy: Curt Marcus Gallery, New York

*Untitled (yes/no), 1991*
*color photograph*
50 x 72
Courtesy: Curt Marcus Gallery, New York

## Robert Flack

*Anatomical Garden, 1990*
*c-print*
40 x 30
Estate of Robert Flack
Courtesy: Feature, New York

*Portal, 1990*
*c-print*
40 x 30
Estate of Robert Flack
Courtesy: Feature, New York

*Passage, 1990*
*c-print*
40 x 30
Estate of Robert Flack
Courtesy: Feature, New York

*Warrior, 1990*
*c-print*
40 x 30
Estate of Robert Flack
Courtesy: Feature, New York

## Sylvie Fleury

*Journey to Fitness or How to Lose
10 Pounds in 3 Weeks, 1993*
*seven video tapes, VCR, television
monitors*
42 x 80 x 60
Collection: Robert J. Shiffler,
Greenville, Ohio

*Current Issues December 1993-
January 1994, 1993*
*assorted magazines*
dimensions variable
Courtesy: Postmasters Gallery,
New York

## Rimma Gerlovina and Valeriy Gerlovin

***Perspective, 1992***
*ektacolor print*
48 x 48
Courtesy:  Steinbaum Krauss Gallery,
New York

***Pascal Triangle, 1990***
*ektacolor print*
48 x 48
Courtesy:  Steinbaum Krauss Gallery,
New York

***To Be, 1989***
*ektacolor print*
48 x 48
Courtesy:  Steinbaum Krauss Gallery,
New York

## Elliot Green

***Emergence #49, 1993***
*oil on canvas*
24 x 36
Courtesy:  Fawbush Gallery, New York

***Emergence #55, 1993***
*oil on canvas*
24 x 36
Collection:  Neuberger & Berman,
New York
Courtesy:  Fawbush Gallery,
New York

***Emergence #58, 1993***
*oil on canvas*
24 x 36
Collection:  Bruce Velick, Mill Valley,
California
Courtesy:  Fawbush Gallery, New York

***Emergence #59, 1993***
*oil on canvas*
24 x 36
Courtesy:  Fawbush Gallery, New York

## Jane Hammond

***New Nose, 1993***
*graphite crayon transfers, rubber
stamp, linoleum block print, gouache
and acrylic on rice paper*
35 1/2 x 32 1/2 unframed
Private Collection:  New Jersey
Courtesy:  Jose Freire Fine Art Inc.,
New York

***Science and Sound, 1993***
*graphite, crayon, colored pencil,
color xerox transfers, linoleum block
gouache and acrylic on rice paper*
35 1/2 x 32 1/2 unframed
Private Collection:  Orlando, Florida
Courtesy:  Jose Freire Fine Art Inc.,
New York

# Lauren Lesko

**_Femininity-Lecture XXXIII, 1991_**
_tassel, text_
dimensions variable
Private Collection:  Los Angeles
Courtesy:  Artist, Los Angeles

**_Orifice (1 of 9), 1991_**
_leather and embroidered text_
8 x 8 x 4
Courtesy:  Artist, Los Angeles and
The Lipton Owens Company, New York

**_Orifice (2 of 9), 1991_**
_leather, thread, wood_
8 x 8 x 4
Collection:  Jacci Den Hartog
and Patrick Nickell, Los Angeles

**_Orifice (3 of 9), 1991_**
_leather and embroidered text_
8 x 8 x 4
Collection:  Sue Spaid, Los Angeles

**_Orifice (4 of 9), 1991_**
_leather and embroidered text_
8 x 8 x 4
Courtesy:  Artist, Los Angeles and
The Lipton Owens Company, New York

# Paul McCarthy

**_Cultural Soup, 1987_**
_video installation_
25 minutes
Courtesy:  Artist, New York and
Rosamund Felsen Gallery, Los Angeles

# Frank Moore

**_Country Club, 1992_**
_oil on canvas with attachments_
34 x 28
Collection:  Gian Enzo Sperone,
New York

**_Pearline, 1991_**
_oil on canvas with frame_
51 x 43
Courtesy:  Sperone Westwater, New York

# Daniel Oates

**_Boots, 1992_**
_neoprene and urethane foam_
32 x 18 1/2 x 24
Collection:  Arthur G. Rosen, Wayne,
New Jersey

**_Happy Workers (Bella and Stella),
1992_**
_rigid urethane and acrylic paint_
5 x 8 5/8 x 5
Collection:  Arthur G. Rosen,
Wayne, New Jersey

# Tony Oursler

**_Road Movie II, 1993_**
_mixed media_
dimensions variable
Courtesy:  Linda Cathcart Gallery,
Santa Monica

## Ann Preston

***Mouth, Nose, Eyes, Forehead, Twins, 1993***
*6 components: beeswax, rosin, pigment*
2 1/2 x 4 3/8 x 4
5 3/8 x 5 1/2 x 6
6 1/4 x 5 5/8 x 8
6 x 6 x 14 1/2
6 1/2 x 5 3/4 x 7 3/4
6 1/2 x 5 1/2 x 7 1/2
Courtesy:  Artist and Rosamund Felsen
Gallery, Los Angeles

## Alan Rath

***Maya's Mikoshi, 1992***
*electronics, aluminum, 5 cathode ray tubes*
96 x 56 x 29
Collection:  Robert J. Shiffler,
Greenville, Ohio

## Michael Rees

***Untitled, 1992***
*concrete and plastic composites*
12 x 12 1/2 x 19
Private Collection:  Cincinnati

## Elaine Reichek

***Blue Men, 1986***
*photograph, wool*
63 x 96
Courtesy:  Artist and Michael Klein Inc.,
New York

## James Rosenquist

***Gift Wrapped Doll #4 (307), 1992***
*oil on canvas*
60 x 60
Courtesy:  Leo Castelli Gallery,
New York

## Amy Sillman

***Ratfink, 1993***
*oil, ink, gouache on wood*
46 x 40
Courtesy:  Artist, New York

***Bad Dog, 1993***
*oil, ink, gouache on wood*
48 x 48
Courtesy:  Salvatore Ala Gallery,
New York

## Megan Williams

***Girl with Flowers, 1993***
*mixed media installation*
dimensions variable
Courtesy:  John Post Lee Gallery,
New York

***Untitled (Red Dictionary), 1992***
*altered book on pedestal*
3 1/2 x 8 1/2 x 11 1/4
Courtesy:  John Post Lee Gallery,
New York

***Untitled (Blue Dictionary with
Little Doorways), 1992***
*altered book on pedestal*
3 x 6 1/4 x 9 1/2
Courtesy:  John Post Lee Gallery,
New York

***Untitled (Large Blue Dictionary),
1992***
*altered book on pedestal*
4 x 8 1/2 x 11
Courtesy:  John Post Lee Gallery,
New York

## David Wojnarowicz

***Untitled, 1992***
*silkscreen on photograph*
38 x 26
Collection:  Clinger/Gal, New York

***"When I Put My Hands on Your
Body...", 1990***
*silkscreen on photograph*
26 x 38
Courtesy:  P.P.O.W., New York

## Kevin Wolff

***Outstretched Hand, 1990***
*acrylic on canvas*
42 x 68
Courtesy:  Artist and Feature, New York

***Arm with Hole, 1991***
*acrylic on canvas*
42 x 80
Collection:  Neuberger and Berman,
New York

## Pamela Wye

***Heidiology, 1993***
*57 @ 8 1/2 x 11 computer images
on paper*
96 x 72
Courtesy:  Artist, New York

## Lisa Yuskavage

***Big Camille, 1993***
*oil on linen*
64 x 50 x 2
Courtesy:  Artist and Elizabeth Koury
Gallery, New York

***Big Marie, 1993***
*oil on linen*
64 x 50 x 2
Courtesy:  Artist and Elizabeth Koury
Gallery, New York

# *Lenders to the Exhibition*

Salvatore Ala Gallery, New York
Basilico Fine Arts, New York
Martin Beck, New Jersey
Jay Bolotin, Cincinnati
Betty Brothers,
Covington, Kentucky
Leo Castelli Gallery, New York
Linda Cathcart Gallery,
Santa Monica
Clinger/Gal Collection, New York
Fawbush Gallery, New York
Feature, New York
Ronald Feldman Fine Arts,
New York
Rosamund Felsen Gallery,
Los Angeles
Estate of Robert Flack
Jose Freire Fine Art Inc., New York
Jacci Den Hartog and Patrick
Nickell, Los Angeles
Jederman Collection, N.A.
Michael Klein Inc., New York
Elizabeth Koury Gallery, New York
John Post Lee Gallery, New York
Lauren Lesko, Los Angeles
Lipton Owens Company, New York
Paul McCarthy, New York

Curt Marcus Gallery, New York
Neuberger & Berman Collection,
New York
Postmasters Gallery, New York
P.P.O.W., New York
Ann Preston
Private Collection, Cincinnati
Private Collection, Los Angeles
Private Collection, Orlando, Florida
Private Collection, New Jersey
Elaine Reichek, New York
Arthur G. Rosen,
Wayne, New Jersey
Patricia Shea Gallery, Santa Monica
Robert J. Shiffler, Greenville, Ohio
Amy Sillman, New York
Carl Solway Gallery, Cincinnati
Sonnabend Gallery, New York
Sue Spaid, Los Angeles
Gian Enzo Sperone, New York
Sperone Westwater, New York
Steinbaum Krauss Gallery,
New York
Bruce Velick, Mill Valley, California
Kevin Wolff, New York
Pamela Wye, New York
Lisa Yuskavage, New York

# Museum Staff

**Full Time**

Elaine A. King, Ph.D., *Executive Director*

Jennifer Adams, *Assistant to the Director/Membership Coordinator*

Wayne E. Artressia, *Gallery Administrator*

Betsy Atzel, *Acting Assistant Curator, Registrar*

Nancy Glier, *Business Administrator*

Bronwen Howells, *Director of Public Relations*

Kim Humphries, *Preparator*

Carolyn Krause, *Director of Publications*

Mary Magner, *Bookstore Manager/Buyer*

Lisa Morelli, *Administrative Assistant*

Karen Musgrove, *Director of Development*

Julia Ranz, *Assistant Curator of Education*

Margaret Sambi, *Curator of Education*

**Part Time**

James Antonio, *Bookstore Bookkeeping Assistant*

Joseph Antonio, *Installation Assistant, Guard*

Jen Bates, *Bookstore Assistant*

Emily Bonansinga, *Installation Assistant*

Amy Cluxton, *Installation Assistant, Guard*

Jill Comer, *Installation Assistant, Receptionist*

Angie Conard, *Installation Assistant, Guard*

Matthew Diefenbacher, *Installation Assistant, Guard*

Carrie Glover, *Installation Assistant*

Kara Humphrey, *Receptionist*

Sylvia Lang, *Bookstore Assistant*

Angela Ossege, *Assistant Bookstore Manager*

Alberta Ridley, *Service Personnel*

Ramiro Rodriguez, *Installation Assistant, Guard*

Alan Sauer, *Installation Assistant, Guard*

Margaret Lucille Stevenson, *Service Personnel*

Allen Underwood, *Installation Assistant, Guard*

Stephanie Winters, *Receptionist*

*Animal Farm* George Orwell *Catch 22* Joseph Heller *The Fountainhead* Ayn Rand *The Prince of Tides* Pat Conroy *A Christmas Carol* Charles Dickens *Murder on the Orient Express* Agatha Christie *The Vanishing American* Zane Grey *Light in August* William Faulkner *Death Comes for the Archbishop* Willa Cather *Slaughterhouse Five* Kurt Vonnegut, Jr. *A Confederacy of Dunces* John Kennedy Toole *My*

*Collected books for*
**The Figure as Fiction**

*Name is Asher Lev* Chaim Potok *Dune* Frank Herbert *Briefing for a Descent into Hell* Doris Lessing *The Old Man and the Sea* Ernest Hemingway *The Glass Bead Game (Magister Ludi)* Hermann Hesse *One Flew Over the Cuckoo's Nest* Ken Kesey *The Devil's Advocate* Morris L. West *Sophie's Choice* William Styron **Collection: J.W. Atzel** *Atlas Shrugged* Ayn Rand *The Lords of Discipline* Pat Conroy

**Collection: Wayne Artressia** *The Catcher in the Rye* J.D. Salinger

**Collection: Eileen Shannon** *Geek Love* Katherine Dunn **Courtesy:**

**Kaldi's Coffeehouse and Bookstore** *Tropic of Cancer* Henry Miller

*The Flounder* Günter Grass *Edwin Drood* Charles Dickens *American*

*in Paris* George Wickes *Half Moon Street* Paul Theroux *Glory*

Vladimir Nabokov *Portrait of a Lady* Henry James *Henry and Cato*

*Collected books for*
**The Figure as Fiction**

Iris Murdoch *African Queen* C.S. Forester *Death in Venice* Thomas

Mann *The Great Gatsby* F. Scott Fitzgerald *Grapes of Wrath* John

Steinbeck *The Stranger* Albert Camus *Streetcar Named Desire*

Tennessee Williams *Bruno's Dream* Iris Murdoch *Orlando* Virginia

Woolf *The Awakening* Kate Chopin *Two Cheers for Democracy* E. M.

Forster *The Name of the Rose* Umberto Ecco *Doctor No* Ian Fleming